Wars, Parties and Nationalism:

Essays on the Politics and Society of Nineteenth-Century Latin America

edited by
Eduardo Posada-Carbó

Institute of Latin American Studies
31 Tavistock Square London WC1H 9HA

Nineteenth-Century Latin America

This is the first volume of studies arising from the Institute of Latin American Studies's annual international workshops on nineteenth-century Latin America.

British Library Cataloguing in Publication Data
A catalogue record for this book is available
from the British Library

ISBN 0 901145 98 X

Contents

Notes on Contributors

David Brading is University Reader in Latin American History, University of Cambridge. His previous publications include *Miners and Merchants in Bourbon Mexico, 1763-1810* (1971), which was awarded the prestigious Bolton Prize, *Haciendas and Ranchos in the Mexican Bajío* (1978), *Caudillo and Peasant in the Mexican Revolution* (ed., 1980), *Prophecy and Myth in Mexican History* (1984), *The Origins of Mexican Nationalism* (1985), *The First America* (1991), *Church and State in Bourbon Mexico* (1994). Dr Brading taught at the University of California, Berkeley, and at Yale University before returning to Cambridge.

Fernando López-Alves is Assistant Professor of Political Science at the University of California, Santa Barbara. He was an Honorary Research Fellow at the Institute of Latin American Studies, University of London, in 1992-93. He is the author of *Between the Economy and the Polity in the River Plate: Uruguay, 1811-1890* (1993).

Carlos Malamud is Professor of Latin American History at the UNED, Spain, and Director of the Doctoral Programme of Latin American Studies at the Instituto Universitario Ortega y Gasset, Madrid. He is author of *Cádiz y Saint Malo en el comercio colonial peruano* (1986), *Juan Manuel de Rosas* (1987) and *América Latina siglo XX: La búsqueda de la democracia* (1992). He is currently working on the contemporary political history of Argentina.

Frédéric Martinez is a fellow at the Institut d'Etudes Andines in Bogotá. He is currently completing his doctoral studies on Colombian history at the University of Paris.

Eduardo Posada-Carbó is Lecturer in History at the Institute of Latin American Studies, University of London. He is the author of *The Colombian Caribbean: A Regional History, 1870-1950* (forthcoming, 1996), and the editor of *Elections Before Democracy: The History of Elections in Europe and Latin America* (forthcoming, 1996). With Walter Little he is co-editor of *Political Corruption in Europe and Latin America* (forthcoming, 1996).

Guy P.C. Thomson is Lecturer in History at the University of Warwick. He is the author of *Puebla de los Angeles. Industry and Society in a Mexican City, 1700-1850* (1989), *'Palagustín', un liberal cuetzalteco decimonónico, 1851-1894 (1995), Popular Liberalism in the Puebla Sierra, Juan Francisco Lucas and Mexican Politics, 1854-1917* (forthcoming, 1996). He is currently working on the impact of liberalism on smaller towns and villages in eastern Andalucía during the nineteenth-century.

Preface

Eduardo Posada-Carbó

In 1973 Charles Hale expressed his concern about the state of the art: 'the historiography of the nineteenth-century political process in Latin America is in trouble... historians are increasingly "moving beyond" past politics to study social and economic themes'.[1] More than a decade later, in 1985, a similar concern was raised by both John Johnson and David Bushnell – and not just for the nineteenth-century: 'The increased production of the last quarter century', Johnson pointed out, 'has been centered... on the social and economic problems, leaving many perfectly valid political ones still untouched'.[2]

This relative neglect of political history observed by Hale, Johnson and Bushnell in no way denies the existence of major contributions to the field. And much has been published in the last two decades in a move that attempts to fill an obvious gap. Yet, despite some advances, the basic message of their remarks is still a valid one: Latin American political history merits more serious consideration. Thus when Fernando López-Alves and I decided to organise a nineteenth-century history workshop at the Institute of Latin American Studies, it seemed appropriate to focus the event on political themes.

The five papers presented in this volume are therefore the result of a workshop, that took place at the Institute of Latin American Studies in London, aimed at discussing various aspects of the politics of Latin American during the nineteenth-century. The scope of the workshop was wide – including topics such as civil wars, political parties, and the use of travel accounts for partisan purposes – but an overrriding concern was with nationalism and the role of the state. Because the papers are quite diverse in their content, they are presented in chronological order, in spite of some overlaps.

The volume opens with a discussion on the role of wars in the origins of political parties in Uruguay, 1810-1851, by Fernando López-Alves. Focusing on the Artigas revolution (1810-1820) and the *Guerra Grande* (1839-1851), López-Alves argues that wars mobilised large sectors of Uruguayan society, created long-standing partisan loyalties, and encouraged the emergence of new classes and a political culture of participation. Paradoxically, as has been argued elsewhere for the Colombian experience, war also became the source of national identification. In the final analysis, López-Alves's paper suggests that, in order

---

[1]   Charles Hale, 'The Reconstruction of Nineteenth-Century Politics in Spanish America: A Case for the History of Ideas', *Latin American Research Review*, Vol. VIII, No. 2 (1973), pp. 53-73.

[2]   See essays by John Johnson and David Bushnell in the special issue of the *Hispanic American Historical Review*, Vol. 65, No. 4 (1985).

to appreciate the origins and development of party politics, there is a need to look more closely at major formative historical events.

War was also very much the state of affairs in Mexico during the first three quarters of the nineteenth-century. Guy Thomson's paper looks at one aspect of recurrent civil conflicts: how the assertion of regional sovereignty between 1824 and 1892 often took the form of armed rebellion. Liberal constitutions encouraged local autonomy – an aspiration shared by all sectors of some local societies, regardless of their class and ethnic distinctions. Compared to Spain, as this paper shows, regional power was more diffuse in Mexico and, as a result, federalist tendencies sometimes led to the partition of 'historic regions'. Despite the centralising efforts after 1867, provincial rebellions remained frequent. Moreover assertion of local sovereignty did not subside during the porfiriato, but the regime reacted differently to the various challenges to the central power.

Frédéric Martinez's paper deals with an ideological war of a sort: 'la guerra de las representaciones de Europa'. Through a careful reading of a literary genre that flourished among some sectors of Colombian society during the nineteenth-century – the travel account, and more specifically the written reports of the European journeys made by Colombians – Martinez is able to identify different perceptions of Europe according to partisan divisions. In the places visited, and in the emphasis on particular themes, it can be seen that conservative views of Europe diverged significantly from liberal ones. They represented two distinctive views of European political and social life. They also served the purpose of legitimising different visions of how the Colombian polity should be organised. Undoubtedly partisan, the travel account was not devoid of nationalist feelings, which Martinez has also been able to identify.

Strong partisan loyalties did not develop in Argentina as early as they did in Colombia or in Uruguay. By the turn of the century, when the first lasting nationwide political organisation was taking shape, some regionally or locally based parties also emerged. The Liga del Sur, one of the most prominent ones, is the focus of attention of Carlos Malamud's paper. In contrast to the *personalista* orientation of the Radical party, the Liga del Sur, in Malamud's view, appealed to its electorate through a particular programme, which included, among others, political rights for foreigners, municipal autonomy against the centralising tendencies of the state's capital, and fiscal decentralisation. Malamud analyses the short life of the Liga del Sur within the changing political scene that Argentina experienced between 1890 and 1914.

The volume closes with a paper by David Brading on 'Nationalism and State-building in Latin American History'. After introducing the rise of nationalism as an ideology in the European context, Brading argues that nationalism was a late-comer in Latin America. In his view, the dominant political rhetoric in the nineteenth-century was classical republicanism. The focus of social identity was the 'cult of patriotic leaders and the elevation of the patria'. Nationalism, in its romantic form, only emerged at the turn of the century, in the first instance as a reaction against modernity. Brading thus sides with those scholars who have argued elsewhere that, in Latin American countries, the state preceded the nation.

With the publication of this volume it is hoped to encourage further discussion of what, after all, remain promising fields for research. Nineteenth-century civil wars, for example, were as much a puzzle for contemporaries as they are for many a historian today. When referring to some of the Mexican provincial rebellions, Guy Thomson points out that 'we know very little of how (these) rebellions... were mounted or what was their underlying rationale'. David Brading's conclusion is also an invitation to further enquiry: 'in the last resort, the relation between nationalist ideology and the practical politics of state-building was ambiguous, varied from country to country, and still requires a great deal of further analysis and discussion'.

CHAPTER 1

Wars and the Formation of Political Parties in Uruguay, 1810-1851

Fernando López-Alves

Thought of as another province within the viceroyalty whose centre was located in Buenos Aires, the area surrounding Montevideo came to constitute the Banda Oriental. The Uruguayan state evolved from warfare and relative economic stagnation during the nineteenth century into a model of civil rights, political participation and social welfare in the early twentieth. The initial period of state growth, 1810-1873, consisted of an almost permanent struggle for control of a weak government which faced bankruptcy, invasions, and constant threats to its authority from within.

This paper examines the initial stages in the formation of the Uruguayan political system by concentrating on two early struggles and arguing that these clashes produced a fertile ground for the emergence of two major political parties which, by the late century, were able to institute parliamentary rule and a two-party system.[1] It concentrates on two very significant conflicts, the José Gervasio Artigas revolution and what I call the first project of state formation (c. 1811-1820), and the Guerra Grande (1839-1851).[2] Socially, these two struggles spawned a highly mobilised society, particularly in the countryside, and contributed to undermining class differences and traditional relations of domination.

From the point of view of political economy, as a polity composed of a single city-port and its hinterland, Uruguay would seem to present a simple picture of political relations. War and mobilisation, however, added crucial complexities. 'Unusual' developments were a highly mobilised rural population in the context of a pastoralist economy that used labour extensively, and the fact that those who controlled export agriculture, the city, or trade with the outside world, did not

---

[1] I have discussed this initial period of political organising in a somewhat more comprehensive account of state formation in Uruguay in *Between the Economy and the Polity in the River Plate: Uruguay 1810-1890*, Research Paper No. 33 (London: Institute of Latin American Studies, University of London, 1994). In the present paper I concentrate on a number of aspects that are not discussed in the Research Paper.

[2] One must add the so-called *Revolución de las Lanzas*, 1870-1872. The term 'revolution' is employed loosely throughout this chapter and reflects the terminology used by contemporaries. Yet the struggle led by Artigas can be so called if by that we mean an armed, mass-based movement that challenges the state, sets the basis for an alternative regime, substitutes ruling elites and enforces changes in access to the means of production, in this case land.

necessarily control government.[3] This was a land of recent settlement that, unlike most others within the region, experienced early and continuous rural mobilisation. The Banda used a great deal of wage and mobile labour in its export economy, whose products included hides, jerked beef, wool and frozen beef towards the end of the century. Latifundia ranching was even more predominant in Uruguay than in Argentina, whose grain exports Uruguay could never duplicate. Given this labour extensive dependent pastoral economy, after the mid-nineteenth century the importance of the city of Montevideo with its port and access to overseas trade, in relation to the rest of the country, increased. Uruguay serves as an example of rapid urbanisation paralleled by the quick demographic decline of the countryside. But unlike the case of neighbouring and very similar pastoralist economy of the Province of Buenos Aires, or other cases in which rapid land enclosures forced rural migration to the urban environment, rural insurrections marked the whole of the nineteenth century. To be sure, as late as the early twentieth century governments in Montevideo were forced to confront threatening rural-based revolts that endangered the consolidation of the newly formed state.

Rural mobilisation had little connection with the numbers of rural labourers. In fact, those who followed caudillos and constantly provided ready militia for political wars came from a scarce rural population. By the time of its first constitution (1830), brand new Uruguay was an 'empty country'. Two years later Charles Darwin wrote: 'I have travelled through a country full of magnificent trees, but empty'.[4] At that time Uruguay had only 74,000 inhabitants, 14,000 of them living in Montevideo and 60,000 in the countryside. The twenty-four minimal urban centres and villages that dotted the *campaña* (countryside) really meant little in terms of population and the economy. In contrast, the small city had already shown signs of rapid growth. It had gone from 9,000 inhabitants in 1829 to 14,000 in 1830. Sharp population differences between Montevideo and the countryside would grow yet sharper. In 1835 the city-port housed 23,000 people and in the first years of the Guerra Grande it had almost doubled that number to 42,000.[5] Meanwhile, rural populations had remained at an overall constant level. Wars had brought much destruction to the countryside, and late in the century Montevideo began tilting the balance in its favour, housing 21.3 per cent of the total population of the country. By 1908 the Banda contained 1,042,686 inhabitants, of which 29.7 per cent lived in the city-port. Urbanisation patterns increased markedly throughout the nineteenth century, foreigners comprising a large proportion of urban residents. This trend

---

[3] High rural mobilisation has been customarily associated with labour-intensive economies, e.g., rural enterprises that employ large numbers of labourers and complex agricultural economies with different systems of share-cropping, small and middle tenancy, and/or peasants. Uruguay had little or none of all these characteristics and, somewhat similar to Argentina, falls within the category of economies that used labour extensively.

[4] Charles Darwin, *Un naturalista en el Plata* (Montevideo, 1968), p. 130.

[5] Juan A. Oddone, *La formación del Uruguay moderno* (Buenos Aires, 1966), p. 12.

continued, and in 1889 a census found that 46.8 per cent of the urban population was foreign-born.[6] At that time, 47 per cent were of Italian origin and 32 per cent had come from Spain. In 1908 the percentage of foreigners had declined to 30.4 per cent; but in the 1920s immigration resumed with central and eastern Europe substituting for Italy and Spain as the main sources of immigrants.

International diplomacy and ties with foreign governments weighed heavily in the crafting of the Uruguayan institutions and explain, in part, the high degree of rural mobilisation that characterised the century. The very foundation of Montevideo as city and port was a product of international politics. The city was chosen in 1723 by the Spanish viceroyalty as a military outpost to stop the southward advances of the Portuguese.[7] Foreign influences were strong from the beginning, and for some the very independence of the country owed much to the leverage of outsiders. In December 1810 José Salazar, Commander in Chief of the Montevidean Naval fleet, wrote to his superiors of the 'undoubtable' fact that there was

'... un plan general para revolucionar toda la América del Sur y Norte bajo los mismos principios ...; que había agentes y conspiradores en todas las principales ciudades ...Que los más interesados en la independencia de las Américas son los extrangeros es una verdad que no puede dudarse y de que cada día tenemos mas reiteradas pruebas.'[8]

Situated between the 'two giants', Argentina and Brazil, the Banda's geography and its small size made most wars in the Banda Oriental regional and international in character. Indeed, until the 1860s all armed conflicts involved surrogate foreign forces and alien armies. The cleavages that divided contending forces were usually related to alliances forged between local caudillos and foreign interests of one kind or another. In this context, whether they wanted it or not, the large mass of rural wage labourers, small renters, *gauchos*, and the rural poor in various relations of dependence with the *estancias* were forced to wage war and to take a political stand. Foreign invasions and constant threats on the property of the large landowners (and that of smaller proprietors) caused them to mobilise, voluntarily or otherwise. In the long run, forced recruitment and dependence created strong ties with patrons who had turned into military caudillos.

Up, until the 1870 the so-called *patriadas* (guerrilla wars of a national character) against foreign assailants were such a common occurrence that

---

[6] From the late nineteenth century onwards, a helpful source on population and urbanisation trends can be found in M. Henry J. Finch, *A Political Economy of Uruguay since 1870* (New York, 1981), especially pp. 23-53.

[7] Three hundred men were sent at this time from Buenos Aires to build up the Montevideo fortress.

[8] Quoted in Carlos Machado, *Historia de los Orientales* (Montevideo, 1984), 3 vols, Vol. 1, p. 31.

guerrilla warfare was perceived in the rural areas as a 'natural' feature of political life. In 1806 British forces invaded Buenos Aires and later the Banda, to be followed less than a decade later by the Portuguese. E. Acevedo points out that British assailants were no different from other conquerors; the *vecinos* of Maldonado complained that

'después de amenazas, insultos, y golpes, nos conducían a los calabozos ... no solo nos robaban ropa, dinero, alhajas y utensilios, sino que hicieron pedazos los muebles y todo lo que no les fuere útil, destrozaron muchas ... imágenes santas (y) en algunas casas registraron, sin el menor rubor, las mujeres por si tenían algún dinero oculto y a algunas les quitaron parte de las ropas ... abusando de otras por la fuerza.' [9]

Constant threats of Portuguese invasions and the expansionism of Buenos Aires after the May Revolution added to a picture of regional strife in which European powers participated intensively. Not surprisingly, shortly after the foundation of Montevideo, nationalism and xenophobia ran strong both in the countryside and among sectors of the urban population. The Banda's subordinate position *vis-à-vis* Buenos Aires, plus the Portuguese invasions (1816-1820) and repeated conflict with Spain, France, and England created the first Uruguayan political cleavages and a strong sense of nationalism. While the so-called Blancos developed ties with the different ruling coalitions that dominated Buenos Aires and during the 1840s allied with the government of Juan Manuel de Rosas, the Colorados established a resilient association with Brazil. Indeed, by the time of independence political groupings – antecedents of the Blancos and Colorados – had already taken opposite sides over the question of who deserved the loyalty of local factions, Brazil or Argentina. Merchants in Montevideo meanwhile expressed their admiration and loyalty for the French or the British.

Therefore, sharp urban\rural cleavage, slack development, and important divisions within the rural and urban sectors were not exclusively determined by trade and geography; they evolved from regional conflict and war. War created constituencies and re-enforced customary clientelistic ties. War, more than trade or the characteristics of the world economy, pushed urban elites to negotiate with rural leaders and created the conditions under which elites declined and new classes emerged. War shaped the new Republican institutions and established the basis of negotiation that made it possible for parliamentary democracy to consolidate in the late nineteenth century. War, finally, created a political culture of participation and lower-class involvement in the struggles of the emerging nation.[10] In most other countries, ideological conflicts involving

---

[9] Eduardo Acevedo, *José Artigas: alegato histórico* (Montevideo, 1950), Vol. 2, p. 250.

[10] It goes without saying that such 'participation' was limited by well-known restrictions on citizenship; frequent struggle, however, did create strong political bondage and a culture of mobilisation that constantly rang a note of warning in the elites' ears. For a more detailed discussion on elite fears regarding popular mobilisation, see F. López-Alves, *Between the Economy and the*

mistrust of foreign ideological currents and the formation of conservative, nationalist blocs were normally related to pro- and anti-clerical problems regarding education, participation by priests in politics and the like. In Uruguay these problems were never a critical part of the political agenda. To be sure, rural bosses never strongly defended the Roman Catholic Church. Only under the tutelage of Bishop Jacinto Vera (1860-1861), who warned of the consequences of modernisation and the dangers of materialism and 'sensual passions' plus the need for a Christian education, did the Church attract much attention throughout the country.

Montevideo and Buenos Aires

Before analysing the Artigas movement and the Guerra Grande, a word should be said about the Banda's economy, location, and trade circuits. The Banda was different from other Provinces of the River Plate Viceroyalty in that it possessed a port naturally better suited for the business of international trade than that of Buenos Aires. When, in 1778, Montevideo opened its harbour to international trade, it quickly affected the Bonairense monopoly of commerce. By the 1790s merchants and entrepreneurs of all kinds in the capital of the viceroyalty complained profusely about competition from Montevideo, and by the 1810s rivalry between the two ports alarmed the Porteño Revolutionary Junta. The 'oriental threat' was short-lived, however. By the late 1820s Buenos Aires was already more successful than its sister city in attracting foreign commerce and, despite the enormous costs of the struggle between Argentinean *Federalistas* and *Unitarios*, Buenos Aires maintained its economic supremacy in the estuary. Its powerful presence stirred strong anti-Porteño feelings on the 'opposite side of the river'.[11] After 1830, independence allowed grateful Montevideo port merchants to resume trade with Europe and to compete economically with Buenos Aires elsewhere. But the development of the Banda's economy remained modest.

Rather than differences in size and economic strategy or the more entrepreneurial attitudes of the landed elite of the Buenos Aires hinterland, the characteristics of war explained why Uruguay lagged behind economically and why its state remained weak. The Uruguayan wars of independence and their aftermath (1811-1820) – which included the Portuguese invasions (1816-1820) and then the Brazilian invasions (1825-1828) – plus, a few years later, the Guerra Grande (1839-1851), were chiefly responsible for the backwardness of this frontier society. Compared to the Province of Buenos Aires, size and

---

Polity in the River Plate, pp. 22-30.

[11] On anti-Porteño sentiments during the 1830s and 1840s among the population of Montevideo, a wealth of information can be found in several newspapers published in Montevideo at the time. See especially the collection of issues of *El Universal* in the holdings of the Biblioteca Nacional in Montevideo.

natural resources appear to have played a lesser role in Uruguay while dependence on European markets, the country's integration into the world economy or the greed of its merchant classes also fail to explain fully the frail centralisation of its state.[12] Not surprisingly, Uruguay, a country with very scarce means at its disposal and an economy more often than not in shambles due to frequent 'revolutions', engaged only modestly in trade, could never really compete with Argentina, Australia or New Zealand, all pastoralist economies that produced very much the same products.

If port competition had alarmed the Buenos Aires elites, the war in the eastern (cross estuary) front during the Artigas upheaval constituted perhaps the greatest challenge that *porteño* administrations had yet faced. By the 1830s Buenos Aires had accepted the inevitable, i.e., the independence of the Banda, and from that point on both ports competed intensively for maritime trade in the River Plate. To the satisfaction of Buenos Aires, however, by the 1850s nobody questioned that that Province had gained the upper hand in controlling trade. Less than two years after the establishment of the first Uruguayan Constitution (1830), Montevidean merchants estimated that almost ninety per cent of the ships and freighters entering the estuary reached their final destination in Buenos Aires. And imported goods brought into Uruguay *via* Argentina doubled those that made the opposite route, i.e., delivery to Argentina from Uruguay.[13] The more cohesive and entrepreneurial landed elite of the Province of Buenos Aires found no serious rival in the divided and therefore less powerful ranching class of Uruguay. Very importantly, while the Pampean landed elite exercised a firm control of government in the Province of Buenos Aires, the same was not true across the estuary.

The permanent state of war in the Banda affected development deeply and widened the gap with Buenos Aires. As the Spanish Consul in Montevideo put it, during every single year 'a war of some sort or another ravaged this poor country', accounting for backwardness and the deplorable scarcity of labour.

'Debe tenerse presente que con estas guerras y revoluciones los Orientales y los mismos vecinos extrangeros establecidos en el Estado Oriental emigraron para diferentes países, pues no todos querían servir y no todos

---

[12] For a dependency argument in which the role of merchants features prominently in the construction of the Uruguayan state, see Nelson de la Torre, Julio Rodríguez, and Lucía Sala de Tourón, *Después de Artigas* (Montevideo, 1972). Although they have attributed great importance to war, Sala de Tourón and associates have highlighted the integration in the world economy as a major variable. See also Lucía Sala de Tourón, Julio C. Rodríguez, Nelson de la Torre, and Rosa Alonso Eloy, *La Oligarquía Oriental en la Cisplatina* (Montevideo, 1970) and, Lucía Sala de Tourón and Rosa Alonso Eloy, *El Uruguay comercial, pastoril y caudillesco*, Vols. 1 and 2 (Montevideo, 1986 and 1990).

[13] For a detailed discussion on tariffs and the so-called 'comercio de tránsito' plus the rivalry between the two ports, see Vol. 1 of Sala de Tourón and Alonso Eloy, *El Uruguay comercial*, especially pp. 48-74.

tenían el mismo credo político pues los años que había de paz era tiempo muy corto para reparar en sus derechos i en los desprecios que habían hecho con la emigración hallándose sin medios para alegar sus derechos y gastar en los litigios.' [14]

On 2 February 1854, in the aftermath of the Guerra Grande, the country was still far from peaceful or on its way to recovery. Again, an alarmed Spanish Consul insisted that in view of the imminent civil war 'la emigración ha aumentado habiendo salido para Buenos Aires más de 15,000 personas en corto espacio de tiempo'.

Domestically, armed struggle heightened divisions between the rural and urban sectors. The predominance of the city, as in Argentina, was riddled with ironies. The city-port constituted the main linkage between the hinterland and the external world and as such was critical for the development of the rural economy. Despite this reality, provincial merchants and rural entrepreneurs perceived the city as a haven of untrustworthy foreigners, a fortress dominated by *doctores*, or professionals, and alien merchants who had little regard for the real *patria*. Reinforcement of these perceptions came from the standard equation in Montevideo of modernisation with centralised political authority. Such talk especially offended hinterland society when its purpose was to justify the movement of financial resources to the city. At those moments, rural resistance to Montevideo political hegemony gained strength. A pattern of rural resistance to the city evolved to represent the Achilles heel of the urban economy. Rural-based caudillos generally opposed modernisation, a phenomenon they saw as both the prerogative of urban elites and the reason for the increasing income differential that arose between Montevideo and the Uruguayan hinterland.

To conclude, the perception of contemporaries that 'rivalry between the parties and chronic civil wars' had been primarily responsible for the weakness of the state and the rapidly expanding external debt were correct. The state's only independent source of revenue had been customs duties and its control of resources was limited only to the customs revenues provided by the port of Montevideo. In the absence of efficient taxation, state institutions basically grew dependent on that source. By 1829 customs duties were providing 77.5 per cent of the national budget, and as late as 1872 nearly 90 per cent of the state income of 8,099,554 pesos came from customs duties.[15] In short, the central state in Montevideo was unable to impose efficient taxation and economic order on other sectors of the economy. By the 1870s contemporaries argued that as a result of internal wars there was virtually no structure at all in the Uruguayan state.

---

[14] Madrid, Archivos del Ministerio de Asuntos Exteriores, Serie Política, URUGUAY, Legajo 2706, 1854-1865. Letter of Spanish Delegation in Montevideo to the Spanish Consulate in Lisbon. No specific number; part of package entitled 'Dirección de Asuntos Políticos', August 1864.

[15] José Pedro Barrán and Benjamín Nahum, *Historia rural del Uruguay moderno* (Montevideo, seven volumes, 1967 to 1973), Vol. 1, p. 186.

Indeed, in 1874 the executive reported that during the past fifteen years alone the public debt had increased about 30 times as a consequence of internal warfare.[16] This estimate did not include major armed struggles that preceded the 1860s, conflicts that had placed even greater burdens on the economy. Indeed, Barrán and Nahum remind us that the Guerra Grande set back livestock production to levels below those of the colonial period as well as marking a return to a colonial level of technology.[17]

The Artigas Revolution

An independent Uruguay was not the straightforward result of fighting against the Spaniards – who, in the Banda, really did not battle the patriots much – but rather the outcome of a complex web of international negotiation in which contending Brazilian, Argentine, Uruguayan, British and French forces finally agreed to establish a state that would serve as a buffer between Buenos Aires and Brazil.[18] Since the end of the eighteenth century the River Plate had been involved in a series of armed conflicts: from 1779 to 1783 a war with Britain; from 1793 to 1795 conflict with France; from 1796 to 1802 again conflict with Britain and from 1806 to 1807, the region faced the *Invasiones Inglesas*. A 'buffer state' between the Portuguese and Spanish colonies, during the 1810s and 1820s, the Banda became a territory in dispute and the battlefield of struggles to annex it to Argentina or to Brazil. It was British diplomatic intervention that in the late 1820s contributed to the final resolution of regional conflict between the Portuguese, Buenos Aires, and the Banda in favour of independence.[19]

Therefore, from the very beginning it was apparent that protracted war between the city-port, the countryside, and the European powers might require a 'neutral' administrator. When the 1828 Asamblea General Constituyente faced the problem of choosing a first governor, they took into account the fratricidal consequences of seeking local caudillos to fill the post and obviated the problem by bringing in a neutral figure, José Rondeau. After that, elites often attempted to lure several parties, e.g, the French, British, Portuguese (the Royal Court in Rio), or Argentines, to intervene. Foreigners were offered either key posts or participation in government affairs by one or another faction. It was in this

---

[16] See table on the amount of public debt in Barrán and Nahum, *Historia rural*, Vol. 1, p. 187.

[17] *Ibid.*, pp. 267-270.

[18] For a fuller account of this period, see Luis Alberto de Herrera, *La Paz de 1828* (Montevideo, 1984); Flavio García, *Una historia de los orientales y de la revolución Hispanoamericana*, 2 vols. (Montevideo, 1956); Washington Reyes Abadie, *Artigas y el federalismo en el Río de la Plata: 1811-1820* (Montevideo, 1990); and Alberto Zum Felde, *Proceso histórico del Uruguay: un esquema de su sociología* (Montevideo, 1972).

[19] For details, see Luis A. de Herrera, *La misión Ponsonby* (Montevideo, 1988, two volumes) and also his *La Paz de 1828*.

heavily charged context of international and regional interference that the 1828 Convención Preliminar de Paz marked the official existence of the country, and in 1830 patriotic groups announced its first Constitution. Therefore, before the first Constitution of 1830, a turbulent process of intrigue and conflict among these actors unfolded. A key ingredient in these events was the Artigas revolution and his attempt to establish a federalist system independent from both Brazil and Buenos Aires.

The Artigas movement represented the only political project that focused on the countryside as the locus of institution building. Other projects, including the Constitution of 1830, embodied attempts to build up a central government in Montevideo which could control the unruly *campaña*. After the demise of the Artigas-led Federation, political undertakings to centralise power in the capital faced serious obstacles, and by the end of the Guerra Grande the central government based in Montevideo still remained segregated from the rest of the Banda. Penetration of the countryside remained difficult. Caudillo power backed by a solid tradition of citizen-militia, which found its roots in the Artigas revolutionary movement, contributed much to the slow integration of the rural areas.

The revolution led by José Gervasio Artigas spanned the period 1811-1820 and marked a crucial initial stage of political system formation. From 1807 to 1811 Artigas acquired visibility as a skilful military and political leader. Opposing Spanish rule, he sympathised with the new revolutionary regime materialising in Buenos Aires.[20] In 1811, Artigas led the patriot forces that put the city under siege in an attempt to depose the Spanish-controlled government in Montevideo. Before the siege, he had already 'conspired' in the Villa of Mercedes, northeast of Montevideo, to spread the revolutionary movement into the Banda. Indeed, the leader and some of his associates personally 'patrolled the countryside' with such a success that 'cada pueblo por donde pasaba lo hiba dejando en plena sublevación'. According to contemporaries, it was not by chance that, precisely when Artigas was in Santa Fe, the Province revolted.[21]

The patriots that followed Artigas in the so-called first siege of the city of Montevideo in 1811 (the Guerra Grande being the second one), composed a diverse group indeed. Ethnically, the majority of his army was made up of mixed-blood of diverse indian, Spanish, Portuguese, and black origins. Cowboys and vagrant labourers were excluded from society at large, but throughout the 1810s and 1820s they remained among the most permanent and numerous allies of the leader and its movement. Small *hacendados* and renters also joined, and in the early years Artigas's troops even included a number of

[20] On 12 February 1811, Montevideo, which remained royalist, had declared war on the revolutionary Junta of Buenos Aires.

[21] For a detailed description, see Carlos Machado, *Historia de los Orientales*, Vol. 1, pp. 40-5.

large landowners who feared the monopoly of Buenos Aires and the interference of Montevidean interests over their businesses. Artigas himself made public note of the support of these landowners who offered him

> 'sus personas y bienes ... (éstos) no eran los paisanos sueltos ni aquellos que debían su existencia a su jornal o sueldos (pero) vecinos establecidos, poseedores de buena suerte y de las comodidades que ofrece este suelo ... se convertían en soldados'.[22]

In addition, nonconformist priests added much to this following. Spanish authorities complained that

> '... los pastores eclesiásticos se empeñan en sembrar cizaña, en enconar los ánimos y alterar el order ... los curas han sido los más declarados enemigos de la buena causa sin exceptuar uno.' [23]

Other contemporaries informed that 'los curas de los pueblos' were the most active partisans of the revolution and that in some small towns the best weapons were in the hands of priests.[24] Overall, however, most sources concur that the bulk of the Artigas movement was composed of gauchos and the rural poor in general.

A soldier and large landowner, Artigas's deep knowledge of the *campaña* plus his excellent military and political skills made him an ideal revolutionary leader.[25] When the 1811 siege of Montevideo ended with the defeat of the patriots in the hands of Portuguese invaders, Artigas and his followers were pushed into a forced march northwards. By the time of its migration to the north the movement still retained ties with the revolutionary first Triunvirato based in Buenos Aires. At the time, Artigas was appointed 'Teniente Governador del Departamento de Yapeyu', in the Missions region, where the Buenos Aires Triunvirato hoped he could re-organise and contain further advances of the Portuguese. What neither the Triunvirato nor Artigas himself predicted was that his long march northwest would be transformed into the most massive political mobilisation in Uruguayan history.

Large numbers of rural workers, gauchos and small proprietors plus some landowners, intellectuals and rebel priests followed Artigas in his search for a secure place to re-organise militarily – a place that the movement later claimed

---

[22] Cf. 'El Pensamiento de Artigas', in *Enciclopedia Uruguaya*, Vol. 1 (Montevideo, 1968), p. 6

[23] Alfonso Fernández Cabrelli, *Artigas y los curas rebeldes* (Montevideo, 1968), p. 89.

[24] C. Machado, *Historia de los Orientales*, Vol. 1, p. 44.

[25] Carlos Machado reminds us that Artigas possessed about '..470,000 cuadras de campo...' and that from very early on (1802) his leadership skills were almost legendary; *Historia de los Orientales*, Vol. 1, p. 40.

as liberated territory. While gauchos and the poor following Artigas named this mass migration '*la redota*' (i.e., *la derrota*, the defeat), Uruguayan historiography and some contemporaries (e.g. Clemente Fregeiro) defined this movement of people, cattle, sheep, and belongings as the *éxodo del pueblo Oriental*.[26] Artigas himself stated that

'Un mundo entero me sigue, retardan mis marchas y yo me veré cada día más lleno de obstáculos para obrar. Ellos me han venido a encontrar, de otro modo yo no los habría admitido.'[27]

Somewhat like well-known episodes that occurred almost a century later during the Mexican Revolution, large groups of the rural poor migrated throughout the Uruguayan countryside following Artigas and fighting for their protector. They provided the backbone of his volunteer militia and the bedrock of his political strength.

For the rural masses the very foundation of the country rested upon Artigas's federalist system that challenged both the hegemony of Buenos Aires and Portuguese domination and came to be known as *La patria vieja* (1810-1820) or *El protectorado*. It was called the *Liga Federal* or *Liga de los Pueblos Libres* and, though at first it drifted, the movement gained momentum after 1813.[28] With its centre of activities in the Misiones region in the northern part of the country, the Liga traded with Paraguay and northern Argentina. Its major goal was to gain access to the port of Montevideo and to develop other ports that might serve as alternatives to Buenos Aires. The political project of Artiguismo was best described by a contemporary:

'Su sistema constante de mantener la independencia de esta Banda Oriental le hizo partidario de la independencia particular de cada una de las demás provincias y de la federación de todas; y así como Buenos Aires había afectado de ponerlas en libertad de mandatarios españoles para sustraerlas a su dominación, Artigas concibió el designio de constituirse Protector de

---

[26] For a more detailed account of the so-called 'éxodo del Pueblo Oriental' and the Artiguista movement, see Barrán and Nahum, *Bases Económicas de la Revolución Artiguista* (Montevideo, 1984), pp. 100-131; C. Machado, *Historia de los Orientales*, Vol. 1, pp. 46-98; F. López-Alves, *Between the Economy and the Polity in the River Plate*, pp. 44-55; Reyes Abadie, *Artigas y el federalismo en el Río de la Plata* and Sala de Tourón et al, *La Oligarquía Oriental en la Cisplatina*.

[27] Reyes Abadie, *Artigas y el federalismo en el Río de la Plata*, p. 83

[28] The Liga Federal linked the Banda Oriental with the Argentine provinces of Santa Fe, Corrientes, Córdoba, Candelaria and Paraná. The Liga surrounded Buenos Aires to the north and east. On the Liga, see Washington Reyes Abadie and J. Vásquez Romero, *Crónica general del Uruguay* (Montevideo, 1981), Vol. 2, pp. 337-63. Also see Reyes Abadie, *Artigas y el federalismo en el Río de la Plata*, pp. 210-55, and Tulio Halperín Donghi, *Historia Argentina: de la revolución a la confederación rosista* (Buenos Aires, 1989), pp. 234-41.

los Pueblos Libres, para que Buenos Aires a título de capital universal no las dominase a todas.'[29]

Rural elites feared the Liga because it represented an alliance with the rural masses; this alliance was reflected in the Liga's *Reglamento de Tierras*, which contained a daring agrarian reform programme that benefited landless rural labour and outcasts. The populism of the Artigas project became apparent in the *Reglamento de Tierras*; land was to be given to

'los sujetos dignos de esta gracia con previsión de que los más infelices sean los más privilegiados. En consecuencia, los negros libres, los zambos de igual clase, los indios y los criollos pobres (serían beneficiados) con suertes de estancia si con su trabajo y hombría de bien propenden a su felicidad y la de la Provincia (art. 6) ... (serán preferidas) las viudas pobres si tienen hijos, y ... los casados a los americanos solteros y éstos a cualquier extranjero (art. 7).'[30]

Apparently, in the context of early nineteenth century Latin America, this federation constituted a bold project intended to benefit the rural poor.

Some members of the old Cuerpo de Hacendados, who opposed both the viceroyalty and its control of the region by Buenos Aires, had supported the Artigas initiative to tax the urban sectors more heavily. Yet their support slowly eroded when it became apparent that the aspirations of the poor nurtured the Artigas crusade. To be sure, their uncertainty increased as the war against the 'godo' was transformed into a civil insurrection led by the less powerful.[31] Characteristic of a revolution from below, as the Artigas uprising unfolded, the movement became more concerned with the overthrown of both the creole and Spanish elites. Its association with the urban-based revolutionary Junta in Buenos Aires progressively dwindled as the revolutionary Junta attempted to secure control of the old Viceroyalty and annex the Banda. Therefore, while battling against the Portuguese in 1812 the Artigas movement had already taken a very strong position against Buenos Aires as well. Indeed, soon Artigas became a major headache for the Junta. In the end, unlike the Blancos and Colorados, the movement refused to side with either Brazil or Argentina.

The Liga created serious problems for both Buenos Aires and the Portuguese. In 1813 the Liga consolidated and in 1815 dominated the Banda. Artigas, now Protector de los Pueblos Libres, enjoyed his zenith. In the end, however, the

---

[29] Washington Reyes Abadie quoting from Larranaga y Guerra's *Apuntes históricos*, p. 213.

[30] Reyes Abadie, *Artigas y el federalismo en el Río de la Plata*, p. 241.

[31] See the discussion on the revolutionary characteristics of the Artigas movement in F. López-Alves, *Between the Economy and the Polity in the River Plate*. J. P. Barrán and B. Nahum make a similar argument in their *Bases Económicas de la Revolución Artiguista* (Montevideo, 1989), pp. 104-8.

powerful forces that opposed the Protectorado prevailed. Besieged by the Portuguese and resisted both by Europeans and Buenos Aires, the Artigas movement had virtually been destroyed by 1819. Nevertheless, Artiguismo and the Liga had come to represent nationalism, federalism, and populism for many years to come.

By mobilising the rural poor against both Montevideo and Buenos Aires, Artiguismo lay down a strong precedent of social mobilisation and political insurrection. It created a powerful cleavage between a rural-based popular movement and the seemingly foreign-oriented politics of the city, giving the already existing rural-urban cleavage a strong class character. The Artiguista army of mixed-blood and regional caudillos claimed now to be 'the country' in contrast to urban merchants, international traders and manufacturers associated with the complexities of the Montevideo jerked beef industry. The claim received support as well in the city-port and within the agricultural belt that surrounded it. It also set a precedent for vertical alliances between rural caudillos and the rural poor. The strength of rural caudillos within the parties and the subsequent characteristics of party organising owes much to linkages formed in this era.

Lastly, the Liga encouraged a strong sense of national identity among the rural population, an identity that had lasting consequences for class formation. The so-called *minifundio ganadero*, ranchers who engaged in livestock production on small plots or sometimes without any particularly well-defined topographical boundaries, constituted a familiar feature of the rural landscape under the Artigas Protectorado. Endless cases of litigation undertaken by these small proprietors to recover grants received during the years of the Liga, remained alive late in the century.[32] A latent nationalism remained alive in the rural areas, focusing its anger and suspicion on the alliance that in 1820 had defeated Artigas and the Liga.

The victorious alliance of the Portuguese, Buenos Aires and Montevideo, seen from the hinterland as a victorious cabal of foreign interests and the urban '*doctores*', thereafter dominated the unruly populations of the Banda. The new alliance came together this time in the form of *La Cisplatina* (1820-1825), a regime organised by the Portuguese. Clearly intended to benefit the large *estancieros*, the Cisplatina lived a short life until another insurrection, attempting to recall rural nationalistic feelings, arose under the leadership of two of the lieutenants of Artigas, Juan Antonio Lavalleja and José Fructuoso Rivera. The former arrived in Uruguay by way of Buenos Aires in 1825 with 31

---

[32] After the defeat of the Protectorado, most of the plots distributed under the Reglamento de Tierras were declared public lands.

volunteers.[33] The latter had developed close ties with the Brazilian invaders which were to characterise the Colorado Party for a long time to come, but ultimately sided with the independentce forces. Lavalleja and his group successfully formed an alliance of rural and urban interests to fight the Portuguese. The result was – with further involvement by British diplomats – the independence in 1828 of the state of Uruguay. With the dismantling of the Cisplatine system, old rivalries returned and old divisions were renewed. The overall tendency was a clear reversal in the gains of the rural poor; sweeping away the last remnant of the Reglamento de Tierras, land ownership patterns favoured larger concentration.

Armed confrontation between the lieutenants of Artigas seemed inevitable, and ultimately this would be responsible for the emergence of the two major parties. Indeed, while the two men, Lavalleja and Rivera, were agreed in their desire for Uruguayan independence free from all outside intervention and for promoting the values of the country over those of the city, they were unable to resolve their most critical differences. The stumbling block was the relative importance of Brazil and Buenos Aires in the shaping of Uruguay. This question lay at the core of the rivalry that arose between the two men, starting a series of wars after 1828 which would provide the context for the emergence of the Blancos under the leadership of Lavalleja and the Colorados under Rivera. The crafting of national institutions, including the first constitution, had reflected the clash between the two leaders and their partisans. The selection of a foreigner as Governor (José Rondeau) by the Asamblea General Constituyente, infuriated the caudillos and their followers, adding to the mix of xenophobia and anti-urbanism in the rural wing of both *bandos*. In 1828 Luis Pérez, a notable who supported Lavalleja, wrote to the caudillo that

'it is a shame that after the orientales had made such sacrifices [for the motherland] somebody from the outside had come to be in charge ...'[34]

Two identifiable tendencies emerged. One was called the *Unitarios* or *Principistas*, principle-adherent partisans, who were an interesting amalgamation of forces.[35] It included many '*doctores*' who vocally supported the Rivadavia Administration in Buenos Aires plus the supporters of José Antonio Lavalleja, the *Lavallejistas*, whose leader had developed close ties with the Federal Party in Argentina. Indeed, most of the funds needed to fight the Cruzada Libertadora that Lavalleja headed against the 1825-1828 Brazilian

---

[33] This was the famous Cruzada de los 33 Orientales organised in Buenos Aires that, as its name indicates, initially numbered only 33 stalwarts. On the British influence and the complexities of the movement in general, see Zum Felde, *Proceso histórico*, pp. 107-10.

[34] This testimonial, one of many made to both caudillos, is quoted in Juan Pivel Devoto, *Historia de los partidos políticos en el Uruguay* (Montevideo, 1942), Vol. 1, pp. 15-16.

[35] These Principistas were different from the Principistas who, children of liberalism, emerged as an organised group in the mid-1850s after the Guerra Grande and attained prominence in the 1870s.

occupation of Uruguay, were provided by the Argentine Federals. Together these two blocs would merge and provide the starting point for the Blancos.

The Colorado party, meanwhile, was a product of the 'clubs' and militia that had supported Fructuoso Rivera. One of Artigas's favourite collaborators and a victor in many battles, Fructuoso Rivera had become identified in 1828 with those who sought the help of the Brazilians against the expansionist thrust of Buenos Aires. Rivera and the Colorados led the *abrasilerados* who mistrusted Buenos Aires and maintained that the geopolitical situation of the Banda called for an alliance with Brazil as the most natural and advantageous strategy for national independence.

A compromise between the *bandos*, the Pacto de los Compadres, created in 1830 a Comandancia General de la Campaña.[36] Ostensibly an agreement that guaranteed a division of power between the two blocs, it also recognised the existence of two divisions in the national space, one urban and the other rural, a division that was an inheritance of Artiguismo. Thus, increasingly, the country split into two worlds, Montevideo and its hinterland. The state uniting them consisted of a few feeble urban bureaucracies preoccupied with administration of the port and some rather remote outposts in a few regions of the *campaña*. Lack of communications and local resistance hindered deeper state penetration of rural areas.

The Constitution failed to quell the growing rivalry. No sooner did Rivera become the first elected constitutional President than the Lavallejistas conspired against him, triggering a cycle of armed revolts. Rivera faced and crushed five insurrections during his first year in office. Later, when he passed the mantle of rule to his lieutenant, Manuel Oribe, he assured himself of continued power by taking over the recently formed Comandancia General de la Campaña. But from there he threatened Oribe's effort to mark the presidency with his own stamp. At this early stage of state formation, the division between the rural-based Comandancia General and Montevideo, and therefore the vital question of where power should be centred, gave priority to the political agenda over development policy. Government could be defined as one of undifferentiated party rule, where the dominant party and the state were almost one and the same. The Guerra Grande (1839-1851) reinforced these trends and set back the hopes of the entrepreneurial elite to focus on development and to control government. By the same token, this war consolidated the parties as the major political forces, contributed to the emergence of a political elite, favoured civilian control over the military and, in embryo, established the basis of a party system.

---

[36] The Pacto also has been called the Transacción de los generales.

The Guerra Grande, Party Consolidation, and Civilian Predominance

Notwithstanding opinions to the contrary, one can argue that this protracted war largely resulted from the expansionist ambitions of Argentina under Juan Manuel de Rosas.[37] Hostilities began when, in 1843, Manuel Oribe – identified with the Blancos and a supporter of Rosas – assaulted Montevideo with a force of 7,000 men and besieged the city for eight and a half years; all in all the struggle lasted ten years. Rosas had made an alliance with the Blanco leaders while Rivera, a Colorado, sought the help of the dissident Argentine unitarianists, Brazil, and the French. Montevideo became the focus of resistance against Rosas and the natural refuge of anti-Rosas exiles. Unlike other wars in Latin America, hostilities did not respond to the hardening of an ideological split between Conservatives and Liberals. As a consequence of the characteristics of warfare, however, the Colorado party emerged with a more cosmopolitan outlook while the Blancos maintained a much more rural and nationalistic inspiration. Organisationally, the war created two different party structures: while the Colorados adopted modern organisational practices that left ample room for ideological debate, frequent meetings and networking, the Blancos remained guerrilla-like, led by caudillos who despised the politicking of 'doctores' and their proclivity to include foreigners in the political life of the country.

The city became known as La Defensa while the anti-Montevideo forces, camped outside the citadel, were said to control El Cerrito, a nearby hill with access to a smaller port. While the Colorados secured urban constituencies in the former, the Blancos were left to influence and control the countryside. After the prolonged siege of the capital city, the separation of city and countryside was strengthened; in the aftermath of the war (November 1851) a French emissary wrote that

> 'Las dos poblaciones, opuestas desde hace tanto tiempo, continúan visitándose pero no se trasladan y hasta hoy ninguno de los habitantes distinguidos del Cerrito ha venido a vivir a Montevideo. Por otra parte, los refugiados de la campaña todavía no han considerado prudente abandonar la ciudad para ir a reanudar sus trabajos o tomar posesión de sus estancias.'[38]

The forces that gathered around Oribe at El Cerrito identified themselves with a strong national tradition that went back to Artigas, Lavalleja, and the 33 Orientales. As a contemporary put it,

---

[37] For a dissenting view, see Machado, *Historia de los Orientales*, Vol. 3, pp. 8-21.

[38] Quoted in *ibid.*, Vol. 2, p. 52.

'Si Oribe triunfa, no será tan ancho el campo para los especuladores ingleses, ni habrá la docilidad de sus adversarios a la política de Inglaterra.' [39]

In contrast, during the war the British Chargé d'Affaires in Montevideo reported that the scarcity of Uruguayan-born citizens in the city would guarantee that the government would support Europe against Rosas;

'... first, the Orientals of ... original stock of Spanish origin do not amount to half the population: second, the legally naturalised Orientals are very generally from Europe or of European parentage, and (they) are likely to increase from immigration ... third, usual estimates of the Oriental population in terms of men bearing arms, were too high and (underrated) the preponderance of the European population of the Banda Oriental ... (preponderance which) is more beneficial for the country ... (thus) ... The inclination of the present Government is to respect the rights of Foreigners and of naturalised citizens. Foreign persons always have great influence ... the goal of Rosas, on the other hand, of which General Oribe is an instrument, is to destroy all Foreign influence ...' [40]

In Montevideo, however, foreign influence would have been difficult to erradicate. During the Guerra Grande the percentage of aliens in Montevideo rose. Between 1835 and 1842 alone, 33,000 Europeans arrived at the port of Montevideo and, among other things because of the prolonged siege suffered by the city, they remained in the urban environment. The influence of foreign residents in the political affairs of the city became apparent. Indeed, a French envoy jotted in his travel diary that

'Montevideo no tiene ningún (medio) propio de resistencia y sin el temor que los extranjeros ejercen sobre sus habitantes ... éstos habrían abierto las puertas de la ciudad y llamado a Oribe.' [41]

European support for Montevideo was clear. The British Consulate in Buenos Aires reported that

'It might be desirable also to remind you that ... in the case of Montevideo the destruction of that city as the capital of a state whose independent existence Great Britain and France (as well as Brazil) are pledged to support, will be likely to call for combined and direct interests, and at once

---

[39] *Ibid.*, Vol. 3, p. 37.

[40] London, PRO, FO 51, report no. 49 and 50, Montevideo, 29 April 1847.

[41] Quoted in Machado, *Historia de los Orientales*, Vol. 2, p. 36.

oblige the English Naval Commander to imply every measure for the protection of British Inhabitants and property.' [42]

Indeed, during the siege, Montevideo constantly solicited foreign military assistance, which it obtained from several quarters. The French, for instance, constituted a strong presence in the city, militarily and socially.[43] Among the forces defending Montevideo (less than 4,000 troops) there were 2,500 French soldiers, 500 Italian, 500 dissident Argentine *Unitarios* under the command of General Paz, the foremost hero of the Defensa, and a minority of 400 Orientales. Indeed, writing from Montevideo to her husband, the legendary Colorado leader Fructuoso Rivera, 'doña' Bernardina expressed her disappointment that

'Aquí ya no hay más que extranjeros, porque del país solo es lo que está contigo. Y qué podemos esperar de esta gente que no siendo de aquí nada le importa sino sus bolsillos?' [44]

It is very unlikely, however, that resident foreigners would have become actively involved politically, either in the Colorado party or in the administration of the city. In fact, data point in the opposite direction; there were heavy reasons why foreigners refused to participate in politics. They did not want to become involved in party wars and retained their citizenship so that they could flee the country if need be. Overall, they regarded both parties as barbaric manifestations of brute power. Regardless of the degree to which foreigners participated, an undeniable result was the emergence of two definite political cultures, reinforcing ideological and organisational differences between the two groups which marked party constituencies and structures well into the twentieth century. The Colorados, based within the walls of the citadel, turned into the party of urban dwellers while the Blancos, stationed at El Cerrito, became the party of the rural areas.

Therefore, by the end of the war, both parties had established constituencies that followed the urban\rural divide. Urbanites were incorporated into a Colorado Party which, partly because it operated almost exclusively in Montevideo, eschewed its original rural outlook for a more urban and cosmopolitan one. Again, although the percentage of foreigners that did participate in party affairs was minimal, the Colorados became identified with pro-European interests and 'modern' ideologies. Contrastingly, the party of El Cerrito, led by Oribe and strongly linked with nationalistic Argentina, was

---

[42]   London, Public Records Office, FO 51, no. 36. Confidential, from British Consulate in Buenos Aires to Adolphus Turner, Consul in Montevideo, 10 May 1845

[43]   During the last year of the war (from 1849 on) several French newspapers were created; *Le patriote Français*, the *Journal commercial*, and *Littéraire et politique* among others, indicating a growing French population.

[44]   In Eduardo Acevedo, *Anales históricos del Uruguay* (Montevideo, 1933), Vol. 2, pp. 148-9.

perceived by many as the stronghold of national indigenous interests.[45] The proportions of Uruguayan-born soldiers in Oribe's camp supports this view. Unlike the Defensa, El Cerrito's forces included more than 6,000 Uruguayans.[46] The forces outside the city walls, as one of its more popular newspapers said, claimed the siege of Montevideo to be an attack on Europhiles and other antinationalists.[47]

Party coherence was threatened under these new coalitions. Within the Colorados, the alliance of the party with the French, Brazilian, and British camps became a divisive issue, and a significant 'nationalist' faction within the party attempted a union with the forces in El Cerrito.[48] By the same token, within the Blancos the partnership with Argentina and 'El Dictador Rosas', emerged as a divisive issue. In addition, the loose organisational character of the Blancos – in reality an alliance of regional caudillos who adhered sometimes to different principles – became apparent. All these problems notwithstanding, the linkages that glued the parties through war remained in place.

The Blanco party included more rank and file than the Colorado. The Brazilian Ambassador informed Rio that

'There is no doubt that the Blanco party is the most numerous ...(while) the party that defended the city against Rosas and Oribe represents, if we do not count foreigners, a tiny faction.' [49]

In the end, however, control of the city paid off, and the Colorados were able to establish their predominance. But that predominance was constantly challenged by the Blancos who, in control of most of the countryside, forced the Colorados to negotiate quotas of participation, representation, control over the Departamentos and so on.

Another very important development that resulted from the war was the reinforcement of strong army-party linkages. By the end of the siege the so-called professional army had turned extremely partisan. After all, the army as such did not fight this war alone; rather, the parties took the initiative and structured the terms of the conflict. During the war, the army split over party

[45] The Blancos, to be sure, identified with Juan Manuel de Rosas's programme of Defensa Americana, which preached the formation of a Latin American bloc against European penetration.

[46] Foreign troops served under Oribe as well, e.g., 7,000 Argentine Federales; but Europeans were scarce in the besieging forces.

[47] *El Defensor de la Independencia Americana*, No. 5, 1848.

[48] This group was not minor. Legendary party leader Fructuoso Rivera was a part of it. Yet the alliance did not last. Shortly after the end of the war the mainstream Colorados allied with Europe (the '*doctores*') had managed to isolate Rivera in Brazilian territory and to gain control of the party.

[49] José María Rosa, *La caida de Rosas* (Buenos Aires, 1969), p. 168

loyalties that remained in place long after. Rank-and-file soldiers who identified with either party adopted the appropriate banners of their commitments and after the struggle openly and publicly declared their adhesion to one or the other group; indeed, a red or white banner in every officer's hat or lapel clearly indicated their party preference. In sum, the conflict re-enforced a process of party control over the military that subsequently only increased.

Conclusions

The end of the Guerra Grande was as international as its beginning. The city's victory was negotiated in a pact that involved Brazil, Britain, France, and General Justo José de Urquiza, Rosas's commander-in-chief.[50] The city was forced to solicit heavy loans and foreign assistance, which were not always easy to obtain, and to endanger its political sovereignty by signing an accord with Brazil. The first of five points included in the treaty with Brazil established a 'perpetual' alliance between the two countries in which Brazil had the right to intervene militarily in the Banda if the Rio de Janeiro government deemed it necessary. It also included the loss of Uruguayan northern territory to Brazil, the granting of some loans from the government in Rio, and the extradition of runaway slaves residing in the Banda's territory. Moreover, the Uruguayan government was forced to accept the use of slave labour in haciendas owned by Brazilian landowners established in the Banda.

Perhaps the most consequential development for the formation of a party system was the accord reached by the contending and now more sharply defined parties. A 'ni vencedores, ni vencidos' formula allowed for power sharing in the national Legislative Assembly. During the war, both parties came to the conclusion that they could not completely control the other; the only solution for the protracted conflict lay in an agreement in which none of them possessed hegemony.[51] The pre-conditions for a party system were henceforth in place. To the disappointment of a large part of the economic elites who sought to direct the state along a more purely economic path of development, the Guerra Grande had strengthened the parties and increased the political leverage of caudillos. Merchants, manufacturers and landowners were of course part of the ruling coalition, but they continued nevertheless to mouth the refrain that the parties

---

[50] Urquiza and Rosas had disagreed on a number of issues, but one of the main reasons that pushed Urquiza into a (profitable, more than 500 millon pesos) alliance with Montevideo was the heavy taxation that Rosas had imposed on imported goods, taxes that severely hurt Urquiza and other importers.

[51] J. Pivel Devoto and A. Ranieri de Pivel Devoto, *La Amnistía en la Tradición Nacional* (Montevideo, 1984), p. 179.

were the chief obstacle to development. Meanwhile, presidents who tried to bypass the parties found it impossible to govern.[52]

These two conflicts settled the basis of a party system and a polity commanded by civilians. Because the Artigas revolution was fought by rural folk against armies of foreigners and because as soon as an incipient professional army was created it was immediately divided by two of Artigas's lieutenants, Lavalleja and Rivera, partisan feelings ran high among officers who found their identity in Colorados and Blancos rather than the state. Despite the aid of foreign militias, during the Guerra Grande a national army or a national guard remained basically non-existent; the contending forces were commanded by Blancos and Colorados.

Party revolutions continued to shape the political system of the country for the rest of the century. True, in the mid-1860s Blanco President Anastasio Aguirre was deposed by the Colorado caudillo Venancio Flores, and from then on the Colorado Party retained power for 94 years. But its hegemony was constantly challenged by the Blancos, and the country never really experienced total Colorado control. To be sure, war continued to reinforce the party system. Five years after the Guerra Grande, the legendary Blanco leader Timoteo Aparicio led the Revolución de las Lanzas (1870-1872) against the *doctores de la capital*, an uprising with enormous political significance for the future of the two-party concord. When the Lanzas revolution ended, the parties reached a new co-participation agreement that provided the second move toward the formation of a party system, a move that some believe to be the most significant episode in the long history of party agreements that characterised the nineteenth century.[53] In the Peace of April, 1872, the Blancos received control of four of the twelve *Departamentos* in the country.

The pact of 1872, however, did little to improve the infrastructure of the state, or to benefit development. Colorado administrations had a difficult time enforcing the simplest regulation in Blanco territory. Rather, strong clientelistic networks characteristic of the *estancia* system were reinforced within the parties by similar networks developed by city politicians in the Chambers. In Congress, horizontal alliances between Blancos and Colorados became more frequent than in the countryside and were translated into joint conduct of state affairs. Such professionalisation of political life, however, could not break the organisational backbone of the parties, which still remained separated as two very distinct entities in the countryside, with their military wings ready for confrontation either to ratify or to subvert agreements. In fact, alliances in Congress were not

---

[52] Several Presidents made such efforts, including one who tried to create a Partido Nacional and another who, when he tried to minimise their influence in the political process, found himself faced with a strong insurrection.

[53] Pivel Devoto and A. Rainieri de Pivel Devoto, *La Amnistía en la Tradición Nacional*, p. 182.

strong enough to create a multi-party system or a single dominant party system. Indeed, as the state expanded timidly into the hinterlands, the two parties remained the crucial linkage uniting rural constituencies with the central state. Presidents without strong convictions and suspicious of the parties nevertheless found it expedient publicly to acknowledge Colorado or Blanco sympathies in order to govern. Therefore, the parties formed during the aftermath of the Artigas revolution and the Guerra Grande remained the most powerful forces in the nation, establishing the conditions under which the distribution of economic resources and state building would continue.

CHAPTER 2

Federalism and Cantonalism in Mexico, 1824-1892: Sovereignty and Territoriality

Guy P. C. Thomson

Mexican federalism, born in 1824, must rate as one of Latin America's most enduring constitutional fictions, second only to that of the Institutionalised Revolution. It is well known that Mexico's Free and Sovereign states, associated in a federal pact, are closely supervised by the federal powers, with state governors, from as early as the 1860s, approved, if not selected, by the federal executive.[1] Yet, in spite of this early centralisation of Mexico's federal system, there have also been persistent countervailing and centrifugal tendencies, associated with local and regional loyalties, to which state and federal governments have been obliged to respond. This chapter represents a tentative and preliminary exploration of selected examples of this local (municipal) level and regional (*distrito/cantón/partido*) level constitutional assertiveness and the response from government at the state and federal levels. The period analysed falls between 1824, when the first federal constitution was proclaimed, and 1892, the last electoral year in which there was widespread regional unrest, before the *pax porfiriana* was finally in place.

Assertion of local or regional sovereignty generally took the form of armed rebellion or defensive secession. Federal and state centralising and pacifying strategies ranged from armed repression, constitutional tinkering, skilful conciliation and cunning gerrymandering to surgical excision and the formation of new federal entities. At various points in the chapter I draw out comparisons between Spain's troubled experience of federalism and its more robust Mexican counterpart; hence the presence of 'cantonalism' in the title (the term used to describe the extreme federalist movement which swept through Andalucía and Murcia during the early 1870s). It is particularly interesting to observe how two countries with such analogous municipal traditions, similar timing of major constitutional changes and liberal reforms – such as the *desamortización* – experienced such divergence when it came to federalist experiments and the flexibility of the state in responding to local and regional assertiveness.

The chapter first presents a brief overview of the origins and early development of Mexican federalism and its relations with district and municipal

[1] F. X. Guerra, *Le Mexique. De l'Ancien Régime à la Révolution* (Paris, 1985), Vol.I, pp. 38-45; Marcello Carmagnani, 'Territorialidad y federalismo en la formación del Estado Mexicano', in Inge Buisson, Gunter Kahle, Hans Joachim Konig and Horst Pietchmann (eds.), *Problemas de la formación del estado y de la nación en hispanoamérica* (Vienna, 1984).

representation before the Reform. Then I trace how the Liberal reform programme, by broadening the administrative agenda, by emphasising individual rights and by provoking major national and international conflict, gave the issue of local and regional representation particular urgency and political prominence (at least from the village perspective). The chapter concludes with an assessment of how Porfirio Díaz, the clarion of local sovereignties throughout the 1860s and 1870s, responded to regional and local challenges once he came to power in 1877.

Federalism, District Administration and Constitutional Municipalities before 1854

Initially, during the 1810s and early 1820s, constitutional thinking around federalism and the municipality developed along separate though closely overlapping paths. Mexican federalism developed from the 'diputaciones provinciales', chosen by juntas to represent New Spain's provinces at the Cortes of Cádiz in 1812 and Seville in 1820.[2] In 1824 these bodies became Mexico's first provincial legislatures, occupying a space which absolutism had deliberately left vague and uncluttered, for fear of the emergence of provincial bodies which might call for the formation of a colonial Cortes. In contrast to the first provincial legislatures, the 'ayuntamiento constitucional' formulated at Cádiz, built upon fertile and ancient municipal traditions. The only link was that the new provincial bodies were at first chosen by juntas composed of the cabildos of the provincial capitals, prominent provincial clergy, as well as prominent militia officers and other local notables (mostly from the provincial capitals). Much like the cabildos of the colonial provincial capitals, the provincial deputations, which in 1824 became the first state legislatures, claimed jurisdiction over, and aspired to represent, areas far beyond the provincial capitals, including entire provinces.

In spite of its roots in colonial municipal regional oligarchies, Mexican federalism was a response to a constitutional initiative from the centre. From the perspective of the provincial elites, the provincial deputations were intended to centralise power over the territories they claimed to represent, while securing some devolution of power from the metropolitan centre. Given the disorder of the Napoleonic and independence wars, provincial elites assumed that, when circumstances permitted, a central authority would be necessary. Provincial and local institutions should therefore be sufficiently robust to be able to confront this central power. But when early Mexican federalists conceived of local institutions, they did not envisage a remote municipality, or confederation of

---

[2]   Jaime Rodríguez, 'La Constitución de 1824 y la Formación del Estado Mexicano', *Historia Mexicana*, Vol. XL, No. 3, Jan-Mar 1991, pp. 507-35; Nettie Lee Benson, *La diputación provincial y el federalismo mexicano* (Mexico, 1955), and Nettie Lee Benson (ed.), *Mexico and the Spanish Cortes, 1810-1822* (Austin, Texas, 1966).

municipalities, holding out against arbitrary power. They thought instead of an oligarchical legislature in the state capital, backed by a strong state militia, recruited by great landowners, and commanded by a praetorian state governor. Mexico's first republic in 1824 was created by a coalition of precisely such forces from the central states of Puebla and Jalisco.[3]

Running parallel to the development of this oligarchical notion of provincial sovereignty, of historic provinces governed by natural elites, now given a democratic constitutional form through the federal constitution of 1824, was a quite separate and more localised phenomenon of comparable importance: the development of new municipalities in the territories of the old *repúblicas de indios*, or indeed anywhere with sufficient population (1,000 souls) and the will to file a petition for the recognition of this constitutional right. Between 1812 and 1824, thousands of constitutional municipalities were formed throughout Mexico, particularly in the centre and southeast.[4] Given the authority over the supervision of elections, tax collection and education granted to municipalities by the 1812 and 1824 Constitutions (after 1824, each state was allowed to write its own laws for local government), this localised state-building represented, potentially, a substantial devolution of power from the provincial capitals to the local levels. Christon Archer has pointed out the important contribution this enhanced autonomy made to undermining the authority of the state in the last months of the colonial regime, as the new town councils stopped collecting the extraordinary taxes required for funding the colonial army and defeating the insurgency.[5] But however much these new municipalities contributed to the fall of the old regime, the new state which took shape during the federal republic owed more to the provincial oligarchies in the state capitals.

Jesús Reyes Heroles and Charles Hale have suggested that the state-centralist bias of the early Mexican federalists betrayed their preference for Montesquieu and Constant over Locke and Rousseau. Although Benjamin Constant emphasised the importance of free municipalities, with their strong communal traditions, independent of the executive power, as bulwarks of individual liberty, he also recognised the weakness of French municipal institutions after two decades of war and revolution. Hence, he saw the need for strong

[3]   Bettie Lee Benson, 'The Plan of Casa Mata', *Hispanic American Historical Review,* Vol. 25, 1945, pp. 45-56; Brian R. Hamnett, 'Factores regionales en la desintegración del régimen colonial en la Nueva España; el federalismo de 1823-24', in Inge Buisson et al, *Problemas de la formación del estado y de la nación en hispanoamérica* (Cologne, 1984), pp. 305-18; J. Lloyd Mecham, 'The Origins of Federalism in Mexico', *Hispanic American Historical Review,* Vol. 18, 1939, pp. 164-82.

[4]   Peter Guardino, 'Governing the Countryside after Independence: Municipalities in Guerrero, 1820-1857', paper presented at the Conference at the University of Texas, Austin, 'Culture, Power and Politics in Nineteenth Century Mexico: A Conference in Memory of Dr Nettie Lee Benson', 15-16 April 1994.

[5]   Christon Archer, 'La Causa Buena: The Counterinsurgency Army of New Spain and the Ten Years War', in Jaime Rodríguez (ed.), *The Independence of Mexico and the Birth of a New Nation* (Los Angeles, 1989), pp. 105-8.

intermediate institutions – departmental councils and prefectures – whose duty it would be to supervise and restore the vitality of municipalities while also balancing central state power. Constant's Mexican disciples, most notably José María Luis Mora, likewise recognised the frailty of the new constitutional municipalities, unable to believe that what had been so recently squalid Indian republics could offer any useful lessons for the new federal political order.[6]

Anticipating this gulf between the new provincial level institutions and the free, constitutional municipalities, soon after the constitution of 1812 was proclaimed, the Cortes in Cádiz decreed the establishment of *jefes políticos*, district officials with lesser powers than those of the now redundant Bourbon *subdelegados* and Habsburg *corregidores* and *alcaldes mayores*. The *jefe político* was to superintend but not to direct municipal affairs (to ensure the publication and implementation of legislative decrees and government programmes on the local level). He had no judicial powers and, at this stage, there was no consideration of investing this tier of government with any sovereignty. Rather, the *jefes políticos*, and, later, the *prefectos* and *sub-prefectos* under the Conservative centralised constitutions of the 1840s and early 1850s, were intended as agents of the central power, expected to supervise and to 'civilise' potentially unruly, fledgeling municipalities. The survival of the institution of the *jefe político* in state constitutions, even after the Liberal revolution of Ayutla, betrayed a continuing centralist distrust of local power and presumed a top-down process of organising representation.[7]

If, by establishing the *jefes políticos*, the Cortes of Cádiz was paying some respect to Habsburg absolutism, the legislators by sanctioning the autonomous formation of constitutional municipalities were quite as deferent to Rousseau. Reinforcing these local and sub-regional (the new municipalities, like the old Indian republics, often covered very large areas) sovereignties, were the informal power domains carved out by *caciques* who had emerged during the insurgency. These *caciques*, many of whom took up defensive positions in the Sierra Madre Occidental (Juan Alvarez and Gordiano Guzmán are two of the better known) reinforced their regional positions during 1828-1829 civil war, when their national protagonist, Vicente Guerrero, was fleetingly elevated to the presidency, only to be deposed by a Conservative inspired military coup under General Anastasio Bustamente.[8]

---

[6]   This centralist bias of early state constitutions, particularly those of the central provinces, is traced by Charles A Hale, *Mexican Liberalism in the Age of Mora, 1821-1853* (New Haven, 1968), pp. 79-92. See also Jesús Reyes Heroles, *El Liberalismo Mexicano* (Mexico, 1961), Vol. 111, pp. 337-409.

[7]   J. Lloyd Mecham, 'The Jefe Político in Mexico', *The South-Western Social Science Quarterly*, Vol. 13, No. 4, 1933, pp. 333-52.

[8]   Juan Ortiz Escamilla, 'El pronunciamiento federalista de Gordiano Guzmán, 1937-1842', *Historia Mexicana*, Vol. 38, 1988, pp. 241-83; Jaime Olveda, *Gordiano Guzmán. Un Cacique del Siglo XIX* (Mexico, 1980); Fernando Díaz y Díaz, *Caudillos y caciques Antonio López de Santa Anna y Juan*

Thus the political decentralisation resulting from the formation of constitutionally sovereign municipalities, which Antonio Annino has called 'la ruralización del espacio político', clashed with the centralising aspirations of the cabildos and legislatures of the provincial capitals.[9] Federal and state constitutions left the matter of the sovereignty of the constitutional municipality deliberately vague, if they mentioned the municipality at all.[10] From 1824, 'free and equal citizens', mostly resident in rural and often remote municipalities, formed the basis of constitutional elections for local, state and federal represenatives. Yet, implicitly, state legislatures continued to regard municipalities as corporate bodies, rather than concentrations of citizens, permitted to petition collectively or to protest, but not to assert their sovereignty as autonomous voters. This timidity on the part of the creole oligarchies, who initially controlled the state congresses, betrayed their fear of Rousseau, as well as tactical deployment of lessons from Benjamin Constant (who had favoured the retention of the French system of prefects). It also sealed the fate of Mexico's first federal republic, the collapse of which in 1833 owed much (apart from General Santa Anna's famous switch of sides) to the gulf which had opened between the oligarchical legislatures in the centre of the new states and the remoter mountain and coastal peripheries, where by far the greater number of new municipalities had been spawned. The collaboration of these provincial elites with Conservative caudillos betrayed their fear, and inability to control, these remote, territorially extensive, and largely unrepresented local sovereignties.[11]

Ironically, after the defeat of the First Republic in 1834, federalist sympathies survived precisely in these remoter 'uncivilised' regions which the elites in the state capitals so disdained. In 1837, the Olarte rebellion in Papantla (Veracruz) and the revolt of Gordiano Guzmán in Michoacán, were both direct responses to the suspension of the federal constitution and drew widespread support from what has become known as the 'liberal archipelago', the area encompassing the

---

Alvarez (Mexico, 1972); and, José Antonio Serrano, 'El ascenso de un caudillo en Guanajuato: Luis de Cortázar, 1827-1832', *Historia Mexicana*, Vol. XLIII, 1993, pp. 49-80.

[9]   Antonio Annino, 'El Jano bifronte mexicano: una aproximación tentativa' in Antonio Annino and Raymond Buve, *El Liberalismo en México* (Hamburg, 1993), p. 186.

[10]   Charles Hale, *Mexican Liberalism,* pp. 87-92.

[11]   Charles Hale and Ricardo Avila describe this process and allude to these attitudes, *Mexican Liberalism,* pp. 87-8; Ricardo Avila, '"Así se gobierna señores!": El Gobierno de José Vicente Villada', in Jaime Rodríguez (ed.), *The Revolutionary Process in Mexico: Essays on Political and Social Change, 1880-1940* (Irvine, California, 1990), pp. 28-31. My observations upon centre-periphery political polarisation are based upon the Puebla case although similar dissonance can be observed in Jalisco (with the Cantons of Tepic and La Barca), in Veracruz (with the northern Canton of Papantla), in Querétaro and Guanajuato (with the Sierra Gorda), in Mexico (with the southern districts and the Huasteca), in Oaxaca (with Tehuantepec); see Guy P. C. Thomson, ' Montaña and Llanura in the politics of south-eastern Mexico: the case of Puebla, 1820-1920', in Arij Ouweneel and Wil Pansters (eds.), *Region, State and Capitalism in Mexico; Nineteenth and Twentieth Centuries* (Amsterdam, 1989).

eastern and western Sierra Madres and the tropical Gulf and Pacific lowlands within the states of Veracruz, Oaxaca, Guerrero (in 1837 still part of Puebla and Mexico), the peripheries of Jalisco and Michoacán (Apatzingan, Colima, Sayula, Tepic), Durango, Zacatecas, San Luis Potosí.[12] Moreover, when federalism reappeared as a powerful force in the lead up to the American War, it was from these areas, not from the provincial capitals, that the Liberal army emerged. The successful Liberal federalist revolution of Ayutla in 1854, which finally sealed the fate of Conservative centralism, was a revolt of small towns and villages in the mountain peripheries of central and southern Mexico, led by veteran *caciques* of the insurgency, acompanied by a new generation of National Guard commanders who had emerged during the American war.[13]

Mexico's *Reforma* and Spain's Federal Republic: The Problem of Incorporating Local Sovereignty

The Liberal leadership that emerged after the Ayutla revolution had learnt two lessons from the collapse of the first federal republic, two decades earlier. The first was the need for strong constitutional constraints upon the federal executive power, which had been so repeatedly hijacked by Conservatives during the previous quarter century. This also meant placing shackles upon (and eventually dismembering) the two bodies which had supported the abuse of central power: the Church and the regular army. The second was to devise forms of representation for the peripheral areas whose assertiveness had made much of rural Mexico ungovernable during the 1830s and 1840s. This was now a matter of particular urgency, for the Revolution of Ayutla had raised local expectations for restitution of land and greater local fiscal and political autonomy. Moreover, these areas were now armed, forming, for a time, the bulk of the new Liberal 'model army' – the National Guard – and thus in a strong position to press their claims.[14]

The weapon the young, well-educated Liberal leadership of the Reform era chose in order to impose its control over centralised bodies such as the Church

---

[12] Ortiz Escamilla, 'El pronunciamiento federalista de Gordiano Guzmán'; and Jorge Flores, *La revolución de Olarte en Papantla, 1836-1838* (Mexico, 1938).

[13] R. A. Johnson, *The Mexican Revolution of Ayutla, 1854-1855: An Analysis of the Evolution and Destruction of Santa Anna's Last Dictatorship* (Rock Island, Illinois, 1939), and Richard Sinkin, *The Mexican Reform, 1855-1876: A Study in Liberal Nation Building* (Austin, Texas, 1979), pp. 34-5.

[14] For the participation of the National Guard during and after the revolution of Ayutla, see Florencia Mallon, 'Peasants and State Formation in Nineteenth-Century Mexico: Morelos 1848-1858', *Political Power and Social Theory*, 1988, Vol. 7, pp. 1-54; Guy P. C. Thomson 'Bulwarks of Patriotic Liberalism: the National Guard, Philharmonic Corps and Patriotic Juntas in Mexico, 1847-88', *Journal of Latin American Studies*, Vol. 22, 1990, pp. 31-68; Alicia Hernández, 'La Guardia Nacional y movilización política de los pueblos', in Jaime Rodriguez (ed.), *Patterns of Contention in Mexican History* (Wilmington, Delaware, 1992), pp. 207-26.

and army, as well as over provincial oligarchies and local *caciques* was paper in the form of a massive increase in legislation and the elevation of formerly piecemeal Liberal decrees into coherent and comprehensive legal codes which the states were obliged to incorporate into their own constitutions. One of the first acts of the Liberal goverment was to order the disentailment of all corporately held property, including that of the towns and villages. Hitherto, the *desamortización* had only been applied hesitantly, by a handful of states. There was an obvious conflict between the granting of greater local autonomy and the issuing of a federal directive that common and corporate lands be privatised. The political instability of the subsequent thirty years owed much to this contradiction, the law of 26 June 1856 provoking village factionalism and challenging long established attitudes towards land ownership and territoriality.

However, it was not until 1861, following the defeat of the Conservatives in the Reform Wars, that state governments enacted their variants of the Reform Laws or began to apply the more draconian anti-clerical reform laws issued in the heat of the wars. Several states promulgated constitutions which went far further than earlier constitutions in guaranteeing local representation and in checking the power of the state executive. The Puebla and Sinaloa constitutions provided for the direct election of *ayuntamientos, jefes políticos,* the state legislature and the state governorship. Local men were to be favoured in the nominations for the *jefatura política* elections.[15] The administration of their districts was also to be beefed up by the decentralisation of the judiciary, with the new judicial districts coinciding with the political districts. As for the *ayuntamientos*, the Puebla state constitution granted them the right of collective representations to the state congress, to confederate their representations, should they choose, to initiate and to vet legislation in the state congress. They also had the right to initiate legislation in the state congress. This corporative representation was seen as a necessary antidote to electoral practices which had tended to favour top-down nominations and the imposition of outsiders. If one adds to these constitutional rights the other constitutional guarantees of the 1857 Constitution against forced recruitment, compulsory personal services and parish dues, and imprisonment for debt, the citizen was, theoretically, protected from most of the arbitrarities of the 'old regime'.

Other Liberal innovations further reinforced these local sovereignties. For a short period, the old army was abolished and replaced by a confederation of the national guards of the states. In Puebla, the popularly elected *jefe político* was the commander of the guard units within his jurisdiction, the captains of which were elected by their village companies. All this amounted to a potentially dense concentration of local and district sovereignty, at the expense both of state governors and the federation. Although the full operation of the constitution was

---

[15] Stuart Voss, *On the Periphery of Nineteenth Century Mexico: Sonora and Sinaloa, 1810-1877* (Tucson, Arizona, 1982), pp. 233-71; and *Constitución Política del Estado Libre y Soberano de Puebla* (Puebla, 1861).

effectively suspended until the restoration of the republic in 1867, war time conditions – patriotic resistance, *guerrillas* and *contra-guerrillas* – tended further to reinforce local sovereignties.

Small wonder that Benito Juárez proved unable to convince many Mexicans to accept his recommendations for strengthening the executive power, in relation to the federal legislature, when he put himself before the Mexican electorate in his famous Convocatoria in 1867. His intentions, however, had been made clear. For the next decade, Liberal government in Mexico meant, more often than not, emergency powers, suspension of the constitution guarantees, federal interventions in state politics against local and regional insurrections mounted by villages and districts asserting their constitutional rights. Porfirio Díaz drew his support from these affronted local sovereignties in the unsuccessful revolt of La Noria and in 'the last revolution' of Tuxtepec in 1876, which brought him to power.[16] How Díaz responded to these pressures is examined in the last section of the chapter. For the moment I want to reflect a little more on the local sovereignties which these Liberal state constitutions encouraged, and also to place them in a comparative perspective.

In Spain, during the same period, Liberal republicanism drew much strength from the revival of the *exaltado* Liberal traditions, particularly in Andalucía, forged during the resistance to Napoleon and in response to the Constitution of Cádiz.[17] On the municipal level, these traditions were preserved in civil and patriotic rituals and masonic associations during the decades of seemingly unresolvable constitutional impasse which Spain endured throughout the first half of the 19th century.[18] As in Mexico, the *desamortización* of village commons (decreed in Spain, as in Mexico, in 1856) catalysed latent sovereignties as villagers were instructed to file their petitions. Villagers not only had to decide internal questions about whose land was whose, but, more importantly, to resolve external questions about the precise territorial extent over which the municipality could exercise jurisdiction.[19] In 1861, an event occurred which historians of Spain credit with an importance comparable to the prominence Mexicans give to the Revolution of Ayutla in 1854: *El levantamiento de Loja*. This movement took the form a confederation of villages, mostly from the districts of Loja and Iznájar, in the province of Granada, organised initially through secret societies and masonic lodges (judged necessary given the restrictions upon free association during the reign of Queen

---

[16] For the rise of Porfirio Díaz, see Daniel Cosío Villegas, *Historia Moderna de México: La República Restaurada. Vida Política* (Mexico, 1954); L. Ballard Perry, *Juárez and Díaz Machine Politics in Mexico* (DeKalb, 1978).

[17] Raymond Carr, *Spain 1808-1839* (Oxford, 1966), p. 294.

[18] *Ibid.*, pp. 130-1, 228-30.

[19] *Ibid.*, pp. 273-4.

Isabel). The movement assumed a more public form when the villages sent their deputies to Granada to present their grievances to the authorities.[20]

The movement was led by a veterinary surgeon, Rafael Pérez de Alamo, with the help of village notables, merchants, small landowners, school teachers (including several recent methodist and baptist converts). It attracted wider support from young sharecroppers and day labourers, demanding land through the *reparto*, and an end to the abitrary behaviour of the Civil Guard. There was also resentment about electoral irregularities and *caciquismo*. In the face of official intransigence and impending repression, Pérez de Alamo armed his followers, equipping each village with musical instruments. On 28 June 1861, to the cry of 'Viva la República! Muera la Reina !' Loja was declared to be in revolt. Forty-three municipalities in the provinces of Málaga, Granada, Almería and Jaén answered Pérez de Alamo's call to arms, and during the brief life of the rebellion, an improvised republican army could count on 10,000 armed men, with as many unarmed in support. Within a fortnight, however, the core of the rebellion at Loja had been ruthlessly suppressed. Of the 600 men tried by the military tribunal, 120 were absolved, 400 sent to *presidios*, 19 condemned to death of whom six were finally executed. The events themselves – the orderly, *civilista*, character of the movement, the respect for property, the emphasis upon liberty, patriotism, republicanism and the rights of man – and the disproportionately harsh response meted out by a military court set up in the field, rocked the conscience of the Liberal press, and even of Queen Isabel, who granted a pardon a year later (but not before many prisoners had died in custody).[21]

When the monarchy eventually collapsed in 1868, the Republican leadership under Francisco Pi y Margall drew inspiration from the ideals of Pérez de Alamo's movement which offered proof of the existence of an independent, socially harmonious, propertied, patriotic and republican rural society – free from *caciques*, priests and the military – waiting to be harnessed to the new federal order. Pi y Margall's Proudhonian/Rousseauesque fantasy was to be rudely shattered. When the new federal constitution was finally proclaimed in 1873, it was the cities of Andalucía, not the countryside, which took the cue, establishing juntas to deliberate upon the terms of their newly granted autonomy. One after another Andalucian and Murcian cities – Málaga, Antequera, Granada, Sevilla, Cartagena – declared themselves sovereign and independent cantons. Madrid, already concerned by resurgent Carlism in northern Spain,

---

[20] For the 'levantamiento de la Loja' see Carr, *Spain,* p. 294; Clara E. Lida, *Anarquismo y Revolución en la España del XIX* (Mexico, 1972), pp. 88-92; Joseph August Brandt, *Toward the New Spain The Spanish Revolution of 1868 and the First Republic* (Chicago, 1933), pp. 217-83; C. A. M. Hennessy, *The Federal Republic in Spain: Pi y Margall and the Federal Republican Movement 1868-74* (Oxford, 1962), pp. 21-2; Juan Díaz del Moral, *Historia de las agitaciones andaluzas* (Madrid, 1984), pp. 78-81.

[21] Lida, *Anarquismo* pp. 92-5.

declared cantonalism to be against the spirit and the letter of the federal
constitution, sending in the army to restore order. Most cantonalist
republiquetas had collapsed within days or weeks although the Cartagena
canton's appropriation of a naval base (complete with the naval arsenal and an
arms stockpile) enabled it to hold out for over a year. Soon after, the federal
republic itself collapsed.[22]

Little is known of the cantonalist movement, which politicians and historians,
both on the right and the left, have put down to the influence of the Second
International, the Paris Commune, Bakunism and Socialism. While some
influence of these ideas and events is likely, given the prominence of the urban
lower middle and working classes in the cantonalist movement (they certainly
influenced the choice of the term canton, the label favoured both by Rousseau
and Proudhon for an independent city state voluntarily associating within a loose
confederation, on the Swiss model), it is far more likely that the towns and cities
of Andalucía were responding specifically to decrees issued immediately after
the promulgation of the federal constitution in July 1873. This constitution had
finally come down in favour of Emilio Castelar's preference for large historic
provinces over much smaller provinces favoured by the more radical federalists
(known as the *Intransigentes*, heirs of the *Exaltados*). These decrees, which
stated that towns as well as provinces possessed their own sovereignty, were
intended as palliatives to soften the blow for those about to learn that the long
awaited federal constitution was offering them little that was new; they were to
remain subject to remote, traditionally arbitrary provincial capitals.[23] This sense
of alienation of town from province was felt particularly strongly in the larger
Andalusian towns, more than in the countryside, which proved largely
indifferent to the cantonalist movement.[24]

The contrasts and parallels with Mexico are interesting. The Mexican system
of states eventually stabilised on the basis of much smaller territories than the
original, 'historic', colonial provinces. Moreover, it was often the central power

---

[22] Manuel Pavía y Rodríguez de Albuquerque, *Pacificación de Andalucía y expediente de la Cruz
de Quinto Clase de San Fernando obtenida por el Teniente General* (Madrid, 1878); C. A. M.
Hennessy, *The Federal Republic,* pp. 230-2; Raymond Carr, *Spain,* pp. 330-6; Manuel Tuñón de
Lara, *La España del Siglo XIX* (Paris, 1971), pp.166-7; Antonio María Calero, 'Los Cantones de
Málaga y Granada', in M. Tuñón de Lara et al, *Sociedad, política y cultura en la España de los
siglos XIX-XX* (Madrid, 1973), pp. 81-90.

[23] Antonio María Calero emphasises the legality of the cantonalist movement and the dismay felt in
Andalusian towns over the Republic's decision to favour the larger 'historic' provinces, 'Los
Cantones de Málaga y Granada', pp. 81-2; Carr, *Spain*, pp. 327-37; Hennessy, *The Federal
Republic*, p. 218.

[24] The lack of support for federalism or cantonalism from the smaller towns and villages of
Andalucía (Pérez de Alamo's constituency) during this period, seems to have been partly a result of
their expectation that they stood to gain more from Madrid – particularly with regard to
desamortización and the *reparto* – than from a provincial government controlled by great landowners
or by urban cantons. See Hennessy, *The Federal Republic*, pp. 247-54.

which secured secessions, annexations or the formation of new states, rather than the states concerned, which for obvious reasons, tended to resist partition. This top-down gerrymandering was initiated not by federalists, who at first favoured retaining, even extending, the boundaries of the large colonial provinces, but by Conservative centralist administrations which sought to weaken federalist, potentially overmighty, states. In 1823, in order to check the extreme federalist movement in Jalisco, the central government secured the secession of the district of Colima as a separate state.[25] In 1830, it was the Conservative General Anastasio Bustamante who divided the state of Occidente into Sonora and Sinaloa.[26] The creation of the state of Guerrero from the vast state of Mexico in 1848, although granted under a Liberal administration as a recognition of Juan Alvarez's patriotic services and of the strength of his *cacicazgo* in the Pacific region, also served Conservative interests since the new state capital at Chilpancingo lay in the territory of Nicolás Bravo, Alvarez's Conservative rival.[27] Michoacán also lost part of its southern territory to Guerrero (the region which supported Gordiano Guzmán), and Puebla, its northern and southern territories to Veracruz and Guerrero at the same time, for similar reasons (all three regions had hosted federalist movements during the 1830s and 1840s). These areas might now be more effectively policed from their new, closer, state capitals.[28] General Santa Anna's creation of the Federal Territory of Tehuantepec under the peasant leader José Gregorio Méndez in 1853 can also be seen as a Conservative design to undercut resurgent liberalism under Benito Juárez in Oaxaca.[29] A similar initiative came from the Huasteca region of San Luis Potosí where the mayor of Tantoyuca pronounced the State of Santa Anna in 1853. This region experienced at least five secessionist movements between 1823 and 1872, variously calling itself the Provincia de las Huastecas (1823), Nuevo Estado Huasteco (1832), Estado de Santa Anna (1853), Estado de Iturbide (1855) and the Nuevo Estado de Moctezuma in

[25] Brian Hamnett, 'El federalismo de 1823-1824', p. 31

[26] Stuart Voss, *On the Periphery of Nineteenth-Century Mexico*, pp.57-61.

[27] Fernando Díaz y Díaz, *Caudillos y Cacique*, pp. 205-9; Edmundo O'Gorman, *Breve historia de las divisiones territoriales* (Mexico, 1937), p. 67. The process of dismemberment of the state of Mexico was completed by Benito Juárez in 1868-69 with the transformation of the military districts of Hidalgo and Morelos into full sovereign states.

[28] Even this dismemberment of the once vast, inter-oceanic province of Puebla proved not enough for the Conservatives who, in 1858, decreed the erection of a new department in the Sierra Norte of the state, with its capital at Zacatlán de las Manzanas, aimed at containing the region's troublesome Liberals, a measure repeated by the Imperial administration in 1864; Antonio Carrión, *Historia de la Ciudad de Puebla de los Angeles* (Puebla, 1970), Vol.II, p. 397. There was a precedent for the Department of Zacatlán in the 'Departamento del Norte', established by Carlos María Bustamente and the Osorno brothers in 1812-14; Virginia Guedea 'La organización del Departamento del Norte: Guerra y política en los Llanos de Apam', paper presented at the Conference at the University of Texas, Austin, 'Culture, Power and Politics in Nineteenth Century Mexico: A Conference in Memory of Dr Nettie Lee Benson', 15-16 April 1994.

[29] Víctor de la Cruz, *La rebelión de Che Glorio Melendre* (Juchitán, Oaxaca, 1983), p. 22.

1872.[30] The rebellious Sierra Gorda, a region encompassing parts of five states (San Luis Potosí, Guanajuato, Querétaro, México and Tamaulipas) was also promoted to departmental status in December 1853, with the capital at San Luis de Paz, in part to preempt it from becoming a sovereign state on its own account.[31] Finally Tepic, the troublesome seventh canton of Jalisco, in virtual rebellion since 1855 under the peasant leader Manuel Lozada, was first offered its autonomy as a sovereign state by President Lerdo in 1872, to prevent it from serving as a power base for Porfirio Díaz, although the creation of the territory of Nayarit was delayed until 1884, the state only receiving its full sovereignty in 1917.[32]

This flexibility of the central authorities in Mexico either to give way to secessionist pressure from regions alienated from their state governments, or to initiate major changes in state boundaries in order more effectively to divide and rule, contrasts with the Spanish Federal Republic's conservatism in favouring the retention of the historic provinces, and inability to respond to the cantonalist movement in the south in any other way than repression. Spain's 'historic' provinces were (obviously) older (thus more 'historic') than Mexico's three hundred year old colonial provinces, and, consequently, were more likely to resist partition. Moreover, regional economic and political power in Mexico was more diffuse than in Spain, with Mexican provincial elites less effective in presenting a united front against partition (although Jalisco can be seen as an exception, in its resistance to the secession of its seventh canton for well over thirty years). Thus whereas in Mexico both Conservative and Liberal (after 1867) administrations often favoured partition and cantonalisation, to prevent states such as México, Jalisco or Puebla from becoming too powerful or autonomous, in Spain Madrid and the governments of the historic provinces were united against partition and any further devolution of sovereignty which they saw as recipes for anarchy.

Perhaps the key factor explaining this difference in the ability of the two countries to respond to pressures for boundary changes was the different nature of the army in each country and its relations to the central power. Between 1847 and 1867, Mexico lacked a coherent national army, possessing instead a

---

[30] Enrique Márquez, 'Tierra, clanes y política en la Huasteca Potosina (1797-1843)', *Revista Mexicana de Sociología*, Vol. 48, pp. 201-15; local interests in Tuxpan and Papantla, across the state boundary in Veracruz, also aspired to create an independent state of the Huasteca during the early Reform period, convinced that they would be able to implement potentially disruptive Liberal reforms in this Totonac area more sensitively than the remote state government in Jalapa; Michael T. Ducey, 'Tierras comunales y rebeliones en el norte de Veracruz antes del Porfiriato, 1821-1880: el proyecto liberal frustrado', *Anuario*, Vol. VI, 1989, pp. 210-17; Manuel Fernando Soto (Constituyente in 1856), *El nuevo estado, necesidad de formarlo inmediatamente con los distritos de Tuxpan, Tampico de Veracruz, Tacanhuitz, Huejutla y el sur de Tamaulipas* (Mexico, 1856).

[31] Carmen Vázquez Mantecón, 'Espacio social y crisis política: La Sierra Gorda 1850-1855', *Mexican Studies*, Vol. 9, 1993, pp. 57-63.

[32] Jean Meyer, *Esperando a Lozada* (Mexico, 1984), pp. 219-25.

beleaguered Conservative rump of a regular army, facing a myriad of semi-autonomous national guard *cacicazgos* spread over much of the national territory. This new Liberal army was, at first, much more closely meshed with local and regional powers than with the national state. Spain, in contrast, retained a centralised army (albeit under attack), locked in a colonial war which even the Federal Republic was just as committed to winning. The cantonalist movement, which drew much support from provincial units and army conscripts, directly threatened the integrity of the army. Spain also possessed, in the *guardia civil*, the beginnings of a centralised rural police force, something that Mexico did not acquire until the 1880s. Hence, in Spain, a powerful central institution, closely identified with the nation-state, combined with more cohesive provincial elites to resist popular pressure for smaller, more representative provinces.

By contrast, partition of Mexico's colonial provinces, if it bought peace by removing troublesome limbs, and did not threaten national territorial integrity or security, could generally count on at least the compliance, if not the support, of state governments. However, the process, obviously, could only go so far. With the growth of liberal centralist policies and ideologies (the influence of the Spanish 'conservative liberal' Emilio Castelar upon Mexican constitutional thinking from the 1870s has recently been explored by Charles Hale), the willingness of federal and state governments to yield to pressure from these local and regional sovereignties diminished.[33] This fear of local sovereignties is reflected in the amendments made to state constitutions under the liberal centralism of the Juárez and Lerdo regimes.[34]

Only weeks after the restoration of the Republic in 1867, Benito Juárez began this process of centralisation with his client regime of Romero Vargas in Puebla, always the first state to feel the effects of centralising initiatives. In Puebla, although the election of the state governorship remained direct and based upon universal male suffrage, the direct election of *jefes políticos* was replaced by their nomination by the governor. The direct annual election of municipal governments was replaced by a two tier, two yearly system. Municipalities were also denied the right collectively to petition to the state congress or to initiate of legislation. The proportion of state deputies elected (now indirectly) from the central districts of the state was also increased, with outlying (opposition) Sierra districts seeing a reduction in their voting power in the state congress. A new district – Alatriste – was created to serve as a *cordon sanitaire* to contain the troublesome and rebellious northern sierra districts. The number of judicial districts was reduced and political districts ceased to coincide with electoral

---

[33] Charles A. Hale, *The Transformation of Liberalism in Late Nineteenth-Century Mexico* (Princeton, 1989), pp. 41-8.

[34] This federally backed policy of tinkering with state constitutions to make them more centralised was a compensation for Juárez's failure to gain national congressional support for similar reforms to the federal constitution in the Convocatoria of 1867.

districts.[35] The district as city state, envisioned in the 1861 constitution – a compact, semi-autonomous entity, with its own judicial, fiscal and military jurisdiction, presided over by a directly elected *jefe político* – had ceased to exist.

This centralising trend of state governments is evident elsewhere. Stuart Voss shows how the districts of Sonora petitioned throughout the Restored Republic for the popular election of *jefes políticos,* promised in the Constitution of 1861. The autocratic state governor, Ignacio Pesqueira, used every trick in the book to sabotage the constitutional reform, arguing that neighbouring Sinaloa's political turmoil since 1867 was due only to the popular election of *jefes políticos*. In fact, the principal cause of political instability in Sinaloa during this decade was the presence of *tepizqueño* exiles – General Ramón Corona being the most troublesome – seeking sanctuary from Manuel Lozada's revolt in Tepic, combined with an intrusive federal garrison in Mazatlán.[36]

In spite of the success Juárez and Lerdo in sustaining client regimes in the central states, and in creating the most effective and disciplined army that Mexico had known, neither suceeded in pacifying the national territory. Provincial rebellions recurred, coalescing on two occasions into national revolutions. Both Cosío Villegas and Perry see this continuing disorder as a consequence of the struggle between the rival political machines of the triumphant Liberal leaders, fighting over spoils, once the common enemy had been defeated.[37] An additional explanation is that the civilian lawyers who took the helm after 1867 failed to reward the military men who had fought the wars with adequate prizes in political posts. Add to this, fiscal deficits and still uncompleted transport improvements, and the failure of Juárez and Lerdo to pacify Mexico seems quite understandable. Yet we still know little about how rebellions in this period were mounted or what their underlying rationale was. Díaz's prestige as a patriotic hero might have sufficed in 1866, but was patriotism still an important consideration for motivating his supporters ten years later (many of whom by that time, if they had fought in the Intervention at all, had served the Imperial rather than the patriotic cause)?

I prefer to see the continuing political disorder, which tarnished Mexico's otherwise brilliant Liberal-patriotic consensus, less as a conflict between rival patron client sets (national caudillos with their regional and local *caciques*), which should, by the 1860s, have been able to reach some sort of compromise, given their common ideological affinities and the general desire for peace, and

---

[35] *Refutación que hace el Gobernador del Estado de Puebla C. Ignacio Romero Vargas del opúsculo intitulado 'Estudio del Derecho Constitucional Poblano' escrito por su antiguo secretario de Gobierno* (Puebla, 1874).

[36] Stuart Voss, *On the Periphery*, pp. 235-57.

[37] Daniel Cosío Villegas, *Historia Moderna de México: La República Restaurada. Vida Política* (Mexico, 1954), and L. Ballard Perry, *Juárez and Díaz: Machine Politics in Mexico* (DeKalb, 1978).

more as a consequence of an unresolved gulf in Mexican liberal politics between nation-orientated actors concerned with matters of state and federal patronage, and a more parroquial element, quite as assertive, yet concerned with ensuring its control over local politics and administration. The source of conflict during the Restored Republic lay in the failure of the federal and state governments to provide adequate arrangements for incorporating these local and regional sovereignties.

From long before the revolution of Ayutla, the centralised political system inherited from the colony was undergoing substantial changes, above all in its geographical equilibrium. Liberal reforms combined with secular economic and demographic factors to shift the political and economic focus in Central Mexico away from the provincial capitals and the depressed cereal districts of the plateau, to the small towns and villages of the economically more dynamic sierras. Indeed (although the hypothesis stands to be tested) the period 1835-1895 can be seen as the age of the Mexican small town (in demographic, economic, political and, perhaps especially, in social and cultural terms), as non-indian colonists settled in Indian communities, taking advantage of the *desamortización* and the expanding opportunities in commercial agriculture. This process has begun to be explored by historians such as Enrique Márquez, Ian Jacobs, Frans Schruyer, Jean Pierre Bastian, who have plotted the rise of a 'peasant bourgeoisie' composed of mestizo *rancheros*: energetic, independent, naturally Liberal, anti-clerical (after 1870, sometimes religious dissident), demanding nothing from the central authorities of their states save freedom from taxation and political autonomy, yet succeeding in controlling the indian communities whose lands were being colonised, and whose territory and political world were being invaded.[38]

The military importance of these towns and villages is not in doubt. Conservatives as well as Liberals routinely mobilised forces from *sierra* communities as early as the 1830s (indeed, finding much less difficulty in recruiting from the *sierras,* given the aversion to warfare of villages and *haciendas* on the *altiplano*).[39] During the Revolution of Ayutla and the Three Years War, *sierra* towns contributed the greater part of the new Liberal army, a strategic reserve which helped sustain the Liberal cause during the European intervention, as well as Díaz's revolts during the Restored Republic. Thereafter,

---

[38] Ian Jacobs, *Ranchero Revolt: The Mexican Revolution in Guerrero* (Austin, 1982), pp. 29-77; Frans J. Schryer, *Ethnicity and Class Conflict in Rural Mexico* (Princeton, 1990), and, *The Rancheros of Pisaflores: The History of a Peasant Bourgeoisie in Twentieth-Century Mexico* (Toronto, 1980); Enrique Márquez, 'La Casa de los Señores Santos. Un cacicazgo en la Huasteca Potosina, 1876-1910', Master's Thesis, El Colegio de México, 1979; and Jean-Pierre Bastian, *Los Disidentes. Sociedades protestantes y revolución en México, 1872-1911* (Mexico, 1989), pp. 87-142.

[39] G. P. C. Thomson, 'Los indios y el servicio militar en Máxico decimónico. ¿Leva o ciudanía?', in Antonio Escobar, *Indio, nación y comunidad en el México del siglo XIX* (Mexico, 1993), pp. 207-52.

it was these areas which produced the most sustained challenge to the centralising policies of early Díaz and Manuel González administrations.

But, who were these *rancheros* and how did they exercise such effective command over their localities ? The precise nature of this growing political constituency is not at all clear, at this stage of research. When all we had were the *rancheros* of Luis González's San José de Gracia in Los Altos de Jalisco, the image was of an austere, bearded, Catholic, patriarchal, economically individualistic yeoman, fiercely independent but politically unassertive and unmilitaristic (until the state forced them to take to arms in the Cristero rebellion).[40] Then came the *rancheros* of Schruyer, Márquez and Jacobs who, although generally Liberal and even anti-clerical, appear more ruthless in their pursuit of wealth and in their cynical use of Liberal legislation in order to displace indian communities or to dominate them politically. Elsewhere, such as in the Sierra de Puebla and in Oaxaca, there seems to have been a greater degree of equilibrium, if not equity, in the relationship between *gente de razón* and indian communities.[41]

Clearly, then, the meeting between immigrant *gente de razón* and the indigenous population resulted in its own distinctive socio-political amalgam within each *sierra* region, indeed often within each valley, town or village. The significant variables to analyse are the timing and intensity of non-indian colonisation; who controlled the new constitutional municipalities; the extent of ecclesiastical and civil *desamortización*; the local experience in civil and patriotic wars; as well as the wider context of state politics. Certain common features, however, help explain the Liberal political proclivitities of these regions, their political ascendancy during the middle decades of the century, and the difficulty national and state governments had in pacifying them until well into the 1890s.

The process of sustained immigration from *altiplano* to *sierra* from the 18th century, complemented from the 1830s by immigration from failed lowland, coastal European colonies into the piedmont and *sierra*, proceeded largely unrecorded and unobserved at the time, and has only recently been noticed by historians.[42] Although the demographic consequences of *serrano* colonisation

---

[40] Luis González, *San José de Gracia: Mexican Village in Transition* (Austin, 1974) (First published in Mexico in 1972); see also Guillermo de la Peña, 'Ideology and Practice in Southern Jalisco; Peasants, Rancheros and Urban Entrepreneurs', in Raymond T. Smith (ed.), *Kinship Ideology and Practice in Latin America* (Chapel Hill, 1984), pp. 204-34.

[41] I discuss some the regional variations in receptiveness to Liberalism in 'Popular Aspects of Liberalism in Mexico, 1848-1886', *Bulletin of Latin American Research*, Vol.10, 1991, pp. 265-92

[42] Arij Ouweneel, 'Growth, Stagnation and Migration: An Explorative Analysis of *Tributario* Series of Anáhuac (1720-1800)', *Hispanic American Historical Review*, Vol.71, pp. 553, 569; Frans Shruyer, *Ethnicity and Class Conflict*, pp. 89-108; Guy P. C. Thomson, 'Agrarian Conflict in the Municipality of Cuetzalan: the Rise and Fall of "Pala" Agustín Dieguillo', *Hispanic American Historical Review*, Vol. 71, 1991, pp. 202-10, 258.

can be detected from official statistics, the economic consequences, being often clandestine or simply beyond the reach of fiscal administration, went largely unrecorded. Most of the *ranchero, sierra* economies so far studied were based upon a combination of mining, cattle raising, muleteering, contraband trade, sugar and aguardiente production, corn dealing, and growing tropical cash crops such as tobacco and coffee. The formation of these immigrant commercial nuclei might displace indigenous communities, as in the case of the Sierra de Jacala (Hidalgo), but more usually would incorporate indians into more intense market relations. Moreover, most of these activities (even cattle, if well penned in *potreros),* could coexist quite comfortably with existing indian agriculture, which in any case, itself was far from being limited to subsistence pursuits. The potential for reciprocity between non-indian *ranchero* and indian agricultural communities was great, and may, in part, account for shared strategies in pursuing the constitutional means for securing local autonomy.

The incentive to establish new constitutional *ayuntamientos*, to expand the local administration, to become familiar with the new Liberal guarantees promised by the Constitution of 1857 and, most significantly for our purposes, to seek to influence, even to control the district level of government, under the *jefe político*, was greatly increased during the 1850s and 1860s, as a result of continuous warfare and successive waves of liberal legislation. The organisation of the National Guard and secular education, the disentailment of the capital funds of villages and confraternities and the privatisation of common lands, were all policies administered locally, greatly increasing the attractions of local office. Federally sustained governments in state capitals were slow to appreciate the patronage potential of district and local government in these remote and inaccessible *sierra* areas, choosing instead to see the territory of their states merely as reserves of bloc votes, delivered by *caciques*, for official candidates nominated from the centre. It is uncertain, however, whether federal or state governments during the 1860s and 1870s would have possessed the authority successfully to tap this level of government, given the degree of conflict which the process of state-building on the local level provoked.

Just as federal and state governments could always count upon evidence of fraud or violence in areas beyond central control to justify holding a new election or calling a state of emergency (requiring the presence of a federal force), so also leaders in these areas found that being in a state of rebellion against the state or federal governments enabled them to take much more direct control of their districts, to limit external meddling, and to forge a basis of solidarity in ethnically divided societies which might otherwise have experienced serious divisions over the application of new Liberal policies, such as the establishment of secular education or the *desamortización*.[43]

---

[43] L. Ballard Perry, *Juárez and Díaz*, pp. 3-32.

The success of local patronage in preempting and curbing Indian rebelliousness is evident from current research on the Puebla Sierra. It also evident from John Tutino and Leticia Reina's accounts of 19th century peasant rebellions which show that the incidence of localised (village based) movements, not incorporated into broader rebellions, was far more common before the Revolution of Ayutla (1854) and after Díaz's arrival in power (1877), than in the intervening quarter century, the period of the Liberal Reforma.[44] In the Sierra de Puebla, the Huasteca, the Sierra de Hidalgo, and the Sierra Madre in Veracruz, village rebellions over the application of the Ley Lerdo were subsumed, and effectively neutralised, within larger regional rebellions.[45] The only exception to this tendency for local ethnic conflicts to be subsumed within larger movements was the Caste War of Chiapas (1869-70), which need not have become an inter-ethnic conflict, had not Chiapas's Liberals suddenly switched, at the last moment, from supporting, to brutally opposing, what was essentially a peaceful movement of religious revivalism.[46]

In general, then, during the Reform period (1854-1876), Liberal regional caudillos and *caciques* succeeded in maintaining control over their territories and in resisting central encroachment. Manuel Lozada's movement in Tepic is really no exception to this. Although tactically Conservative at times, from its proclamations it was a fairly orthodox Liberal-federalist movement, concerned about issues of local autonomy, local control over the *reparto* and involving a coalition between a non-Indian peasant bourgeoisie (such as Lozada himself) and Indian communities.[47] These coalitions, shielded by Mexico's tangled topography, explain the continuing weakness of the centre in confronting rebellious regions. Popular Liberal movements on the *altiplano*, by contrast, proved shortlived. The *reparto* inspired peasant movements which occurred on the *altiplano* in 1868-69 – in Chalco, Puebla and the Mezquital – attracted some urban, ideologically sophisticated leaders, but failed to receive the kind of patronage from broader Liberal armed movements which was available in the less accessible Sierras. On the *altiplano*, the presence of the hacienda, the lack of a land surplus and the availability of defence forces from the towns, quickly suffocated armed popular movements.[48]

---

[44] Leticia Reina, *Las rebeliones campesinas*; John Tutino, *From Insurrection to Revolution in Mexico: Social Bases of Agrarian Violence in Mexico, 1750-1940* (Princeton, 1986), pp. 215-8.

[45] Guy P. C. Thomson, 'Agrarian Conflict', pp. 226-42; Michael T. Ducey, 'Tierras comunales y rebeliones en el norte de Veracruz', pp. 209-29.

[46] Jan Rus, 'Whose Caste War? Indians, Ladinos and the Chiapas "Caste War" of 1869', in *Spaniards and Indians in Southeastern Mesomamerica* (Lincoln, Neb., 1983), pp.127-60.

[47] Jean Meyer, *La tierra de Manuel Lozada* (Mexico, 1989).

[48] For the limits of Liberal village mobilisation in the sugar zones of Morelos during the aftermath of the revolution of Ayutla, see Leticia Reina, *Las rebeliones campesinas*, pp. 64-83,132-5, 255-69; John Tutino, 'Agrarian Social Change and Peasant Rebellion in Nineteenth-Century Mexico: The Example of Chalco'; Friedrich Katz, *Riot, Rebellion and Revolution Rural Social Conflict in Mexico* (Princeton, 1988), pp. 95-140; and Florencia Mallon, 'Peasants and State Formation in Nineteenth-

The last chance (before the revolution of 1910) for these central plateau regions to receive some official attention came in 1876, when Díaz and many other military commanders promised to attend to the agrarian concerns of *altiplano* villages, in exchange for military support during the Revolution of Tuxtepec.[49] However, it was the National Guard from the Sierras which provided the bulk of the *Ejército Regenerador de la Libertad*. The list of National Guard companies garrisoning Mexico City for three months following Díaz's victory at Tecoac reads like a political geography of such regions, with units drawn from an archipelago spanning the Sierras of Hidalgo, Puebla, Veracruz, Oaxaca and Guerrero.[50]

The success of the revolution of Tuxtepec was due to the ability of these areas to generate the cash and supplies for sustaining the revolt for almost a year while the federal army ultimately was starved of funds. The seemingly limitless fiscal potential of *sierra* areas – borne out by the monthly remittance of prodigous amounts of cash, maize dough (*totopo*), sugar loaf (*panela*), *aguardiente, chilpotle* pepper and coffee from the remotest hamlet -- is the most visible demonstration of the authority *sierra* towns exercised over subject communities, contrasting vividly with the still tenuous control federal and state governments exercised over their territories.[51] It was this unique combination of possessing *elementos propios,* seasoned military units, under popular commanders, with networks of command and obedience over wide areas, reinforced by powerful personal ties of reciprocity (credit, *compadrazgo*, masonic pledges, etc.), which enabled Mexican *serrano* leaders to pose such a formidable challenge to state governments and to the federation from the 1830s until the 1870s.

Díaz and Regional and Local Challenges

With Díaz's victory, would the local sovereignties which had brought him to power now reach a truce with the centralising state and federal powers which had so consistently ignored their consititutional rights during the Restored Republic? Both the Plan de la Noria and the Plan de Tuxtepec had been explicit about the need for municipal sovereignty. The Plan de la Noria had declared that:

---

century Mexico: Morelos 1848-1858', *Political Power and Social Theory*, Vol. 7, 1988, pp. 1-54.

[49] Gastón García Cantú, *Historia del Socialismo en México, Siglos XIX* (Mexico, 1969), pp. 72, 437.

[50] *Memoria Presentada al Congreso de la Unión Por el Secretario de Estado y del Despacho de Guerra y Marina de la República Mexicana* (Mexico, 1878), pp. 125-35.

[51] For the provision of war supplies from the Sierra de Puebla during the revolts of La Noria and Tuxtepec see Guy P. C. Thomson, 'The District as City-State, Tetela de Ocampo and its Territory, 1869-1889', paper presented at the Conference at the University of Texas, Austin, 'Culture, Power and Politics in Nineteenth Century Mexico: A Conference in Memory of Dr Nettie Lee Benson', 15-16 April 1994.

'"Constitución de 1857 y libertad electoral" será nuestra bandera, "menos gobierno y mas libertades" nuestro programa....la unión garantice a los ayuntamientos derechos y recursos propios, como elementos indispensables para su libertad y independencia...'[52]

The Plan de Tuxtepec made even more of the need to guarantee municipal freedom and sovereignty from executive interference.[53]

For a short time, the chieftains of the Puebla Sierra, Generals Juan N Méndez and Juan C Bonilla, two of the principal exponents of vesting districts and municipalities with greater powers, occupied the presidential seat and the presidency of the federal chamber of deputies. Méndez insisted that the original 1861 state constitution, with its direct popular elections for *ayuntamientos* and *jefes políticos,* be restored in its entirety. Bonilla, in his inaugural speech to the federal congress, asserted that:

'era el pueblo que manifestaba su soberana voluntad contra la oligarquía del menor número; era el pueblo que rompía los grillos impuestos por las absurdas leyes de municipio...'[54]

There was much talk in the Puebla state and federal congresses at this time about the municipalities becoming a 'fourth power'.[55]

Soon, however, the process of centralisation of federal and state executive power recommenced. It is particularly interesting to observe how this process occurred in Puebla, a state in which radical Liberal *tuxtepecanos* (Bonilla 1877-1880, then Méndez 1880-1884) held power during first the two post-Tuxtepec administrations. Once in power, Bonilla kept to his word by reintroducing the 1861 constitution and attempting, for a short period, to initiate constitutional reforms which would have made the *ayuntamientos* a fourth power.[56] However, the experience of direct elections at all levels of administration proved to be so disruptive of the now much lauded 'order' that, by the end of the decade, *jefes políticos* were once more being appointed by the governor. Indeed, in 1879, the president of the state's supreme court, León Guzmán (a veteran *constituyente* of

---

[52] The Plan de la Noria was attacked in the official *poblano* press: 'Ni á Prudhon, ni á Furrier, ni á ningún comunista, se le pudo haber ocurrido semejante teoría...', *Periódico Oficial*, Vol.II, No. 89, 16 November 1871.

[53] *Periódico Oficial*, Vol. VIII, No.1, 25 November 1876.

[54] *Periódico Oficial*, Vol. VIII, No. 38, 7 April 1877, p.3.

[55] For *tuxtepecano* radicalism and its impact upon municipal elections in the federal capital, see Daniel Cosío Villegas, *Historia Moderna de México: El Porfiriato. La Vida Política Interior. Parte Primera* (Mexico, 1970), pp. 400-6, 442-54; Charles Hale also touches on the expectations of municipal reform in *The Transformation of Liberalism*, pp. 57, 91, 223.

[56] *Periódico Oficial*, Vol.VIII, No. 61, 27 June 1877.

1856 and, in 1867, as governor of the state of Guanajuato, one of the principal opponents – along with Méndez – of Juárez's centralising *convocatoria*) claimed that the municipal presidents had degenerated to become mere agents of centrally appounted *jefes políticos*.[57] Bonilla's conversion to a centralist position was demonstrated in 1879 in his hostile response to a peaceful movement of villages at Texmelucan (close to the state capital), invoking the ideals of the Revolution of Tuxtepec and requesting land through the *reparto*, led by his former companion at arms, Alberto de Santa Fe. Without any apparent hesitation, Bonilla allowed a federal force swiftly to suppress a movement which he described as 'una asonada comunista'.[58]

General Méndez, Bonilla's *serrano* successor in the state governorship, attempted to strike a balance between the governor's right to vigilate municipalities through the *jefes políticos* and the need for the *ayuntamientos* to take an active part in matters of local concern. In a proposal for constitutional reform put forward in 1883, shortly before he was removed from the state by Díaz, Méndez sought to restore the balance between the now centrally imposed, *jefes políticos*, and their subject municipalities. *Ayuntamientos* would regain the right to initiate legislation in the state congress, to be consulted on boundary changes, to approve any constitutional changes (with three *municipios* in combination being empowered to inititiate constitutional changes) and to become established, providing the new *ayuntamiento* was able to demonstrate a population of at least 5,000 souls (4,000 more than had been required by the constitution of Cádiz in 1812).[59] This last *serrano* initiative, before Puebla was invaded by the federal army in 1884, beginning a twenty-five year dynasty of northern generals imposed by Díaz upon the state, represents an interesting return to the early, post-Cádiz period of more active municipal corporations, that were expected to seek direct representation before the provincial executives and legislatures. Behind the proposal, however, was a presumption that the post-Cádiz democratic channels had been failing in this task. For General Méndez, the reform was directed both at restoring his authority in the *municipios,* particularly among village national guard commanders and school teachers, who, together, formed the basis of his *cacicazgo* in the north of the state, as well as at undermining the work of federal agents, infiltrating district and municipal politics, preparing the ground for the election of Díaz's nominee, General Rosendo Márquez, for the state governorship.[60]

---

[57] León Guzmán, *Algunas observaciones contra el monstruoso proyecto de reforma a la Constitución del Estado* (Puebla, 1879).

[58] García Cantú, *El Socialismo en Mexico*, pp. 220-34, 480-1.

[59] Secretaría del Congreso del Estado L. y S de Puebla, *Proyecto de reformas a la Constitución del estado, aprobado por la Cámara en la sesión del día 4 de julio de 1883* (Puebla, 1883).

[60] María del Carmen Ruiz de la Garza, 'Elecciones en el Estado de Puebla (1884)', in *Catálogo de Documentos – Carta de la Colección Porfirio Díaz* (Mexico, 1987), pp. xxix-liii; D. Cosío Villegas, *Historia Moderna de México: El Porfiriato. La Vida Política Interior. Parte Primera*, pp. 623-7.

A similar federal intervention occurred in Sonora in 1883 where, since 1881, the extreme federalist, Carlos C Ortiz, had occupied the governorship, astutely playing off three sets of federal influences (Manuel González, the encumbent president, Porfirio Díaz, preparing his return to the presidency, and the commander of the federal division currently engaged in suppressing the Yaqui autonomist movement under José María Leyva – *alias* Cajeme). In 1880, Ortiz had finally restored the election of *jefes políticos*, sought by Sonora's municipalities since 1867. Cajeme was elected as one such *jefe político*, demonstrating the utility of permitting a strong element of sovereignty at the district level, in regions with a cohesive and potentially agressive indian population.[61] A similar arrangement was reached at the same time in Campeche where the state government guaranteed to the formerly rebellious *cacicazgo* of Ixkanha its autonomy and the right to maintain a militarised social structure, provided the cacique adopted the title of *jefe político*, used the seal of the eagle on his correspondence and denied support to the Maya rebels further to east.[62]

While this arrangement in Campeche served to keep the peace until well into this century, in Sonora the federal force under Generals Carbó and Reyes was determined to prosecute the war against the *indios bravos*, principally the Apaches, but among whom were also lumped the Yaqui *indios mansos*, under Cajeme. The removal of Carlos Ortiz by General Bernardo Reyes, and his replacement by the indian fighter Luis Torres, served the dual purpose of strengthening federal control over this remote but strategically important state, and in suffocating, for good, a model of district sovereignty which would have served to keep the peace (but with the disadvantage that the Yaquis would have remained in control of Sonora's best agricultural lands).[63]

But what more general patterns can be observed in Porfirio Díaz's response to regional and sub-regional political assertiveness? Recent studies of state and regional politics have begun to reveal a wide range of federal strategies designed to ensure order in the states.[64] Before his reelection in 1884, Díaz's authority

---

[61] Don Coerver, 'Federal-State Relations during the Porfiriato. The Case of Sonora, 1879-1884', *The Americas*, Vol. 33, 1976-7; Evelyn Hu-DeHart, 'Peasant Rebellion in the Northwest: The Yaqui Indians of Sonora, 1740-1976', in Katz, *Riot, Rebellion and Revolution*, pp.160-1, D. Cosío Villegas, *Historia Moderna de México: El Porfiriato. La Vida Política Interior. Parte Primera*, pp. 604-15.

[62] Alfonso Villa Rojas, *The Maya of East Central Quintana Roo* (Washington DC, 1945,) pp. 25-6.

[63] Don Coerver, 'Federal-State Relations'.

[64] Raymond Buve, 'Transformación y patronazgo político en el México rural; continuidad y cambio entre 1867 y 1920', in Antonio Annino (ed.), *El Liberalismo en México* (Hamburg, 1993); pp.143-76; Romana Falcón, 'La desaparición de los jefes políticos en Coahuila. Una paradoja porfiriana', *Historia Mexicana*, Vol. 147, 1988, pp. 423-67; Romana Falcón, 'Jefes Políticos y rebeliones campesinas: Uso y abuso del poder en el estado de México', in Jaime Ródriguez (ed.), *Patterns of Contention in Mexican History* (Wilmington, Del., 1992), pp. 243-74; Friedrich Katz (ed.), *Porfirio Díaz frente al descontento popular regional (1891-1893)* (Mexico, 1986); William Stanley Langston, 'Coahuila; Centralisation against State Autonomy', in Thomas Benjamin and William McNellie, *Other Mexicos: Essays on Mexican Regional History, 1876-1911* (Albuquerque, 1984).

was inadequate, either for protecting or for confronting regional *caciques*. Such was the case in the north of the country, where the toppling of Carlos Ortiz in 1882, Díaz's preferred candidate in Sonora, illustrated his weakness at this stage.[65] With Díaz's return to the presidency in 1884, two broad patterns of federal response to local assertiveness can be detected: the first, an authoritarian, centralising tendency in dealing with those movements which threatened the stability of federal politics (particularly in periods coinciding with the presidential reelection), and the second, a pragmatic, low profile, moderating tendency in dealing with regional assertiveness which only threatened the stability of politics in a single state, with the federal government using its network of agents with the aim of restoring equilibrium.

A good example of the first kind of response can be found in the attempt (mentioned earlier) by General Juan N Méndez to have his son, Miguel, elected as his successor to the Puebla governorship in 1884. Díaz responded by sentencing his old companion at arms to perpetual internal exile from the state of Puebla and certain death if he chose to return to his bailiwick in the Puebla Sierra. On two occasions, Méndez had convoked conventions of state governors to deliberate upon presidential candidates, and Díaz evidently distrusted such 'extra-territorial' ambitions, also fearing perhaps that Méndez would take over Díaz's traditional role as the Cincinnatus of the Mexican southeast.[66]

If Díaz's 'promotion' of Méndez from his Puebla *cacicazgo* to the presidency of the Supreme Court of Military Justice was conducted with consummate skill and tact, his treatment of General Trinidad García de la Cadena (former Governor of Zacatecas), was altogether more ruthless. General García repeated the error committed by his father, Francisco García y Salinas, half a century earlier, who had paid with his life while leading a confederation of Liberal federalist states against a resurgent centralism in 1835.[67] The son's crime was more modest, but the stakes in 1880s were higher. In 1884, García de la Cadena had convened a junta of governors from the north west central region (Sinaloa, Durango, Zacatecas, San Luis Potosí and Jalisco), in consultation with urban labour leaders, to deliberate upon the nomination of a *tuxtepecano* for the presidential succession. What concerned Díaz in this instance, apart from the uninvited intrusion into what was becoming the most sacred of Mexican rituals, was the evidence that García de la Cadena's initiative was linked to a rash of rural disturbances throughout the republic at this time (provoked in Puebla, at least, by the demotion of the National Guard of the states to auxiliary status

---

[65] Don Coerver, 'Federal-State Relations', pp. 576-9.

[66] D. Cosío Villegas, *Historia Moderna de México: El Porfiriato, La Vida Política Interior. Parte Primera*, pp. 623-27.

[67] Michael Costeloe, *The Central Republic in Mexico 1835-1846* (Cambridge, 1993), p. 51.

within the federal army).[68] Two years later, disgusted by the new centralised
order, García de la Cadena plotted a rebellion with fellow *tuxtepecano* generals
from the northwest centre. In October 1886, anticipating a *pronunciamiento*
from the Zacatecas caudillo, Díaz ordered this old companion to be detained in
Zacatecas.[69] Who ordered García's execution at a railway station in Zacatecas,
while this prestigious military hero was loyally awaiting the train to take him to
Mexico for trial is still debated in Mexico. It was a stunning demonstration that
the age of the legitimate provincial rebellion was ended.

What is interesting about Trinidad García's challenge to Díaz's leadership
from north-west central Mexico, was the kaleidoscope of regional and local
movements the movement embraced. One of the most persistent of these was led
by Heraclio Bernal, who first achieved national renown for his spectacular
assaults upon silver *conductas* traversing central and southern Sinaloa from
Zacatecas and Durango. During the late 1870s, Bernal graduated from banditry
to supporting a rebellion against the federally imposed state governor General
Cañedo, led by Jesús Ramírez Terrón, a popular candidate for the governorship
who felt defrauded of victory. After the defeat of Ramírez Terrón, Bernal faced
unremitting persecution from Cañedo (backed by federal forces) until, following
the capture of his two brothers in December 1885, Bernal agreed to enter
negotiations with the governor.

The terms of an amnesty proposed by Bernal, and accepted by governor
Cañedo and the federal commander, General Rubi, are revealing. Bernal would
lay down his arms on the condition that he was appointed *director político* of the
municipality of Otáez, paid 30,000 pesos for attending to his costs, and allowed
to retain a force of up to thirty men. Although acceptable to all three parties in
Sinaloa, the terms of the amnesty were soon rejected by the Ministry of War,
which remained intent upon crushing this Jacobin vestige of disobedience.
Bernal was therefore obliged to remain a rebel, in order to resist renewed
federal and state campaigns of pacification. Finally, in 1887, after the death of
García de la Cadena (who had anticipated support from Bernal in his challenge
to Díaz), from his base in Sinaloa's Sierra de Conitaca, Bernal issued his first
detailed revolutionary project: the Plan de Conitaca. There is some evidence that
Bernal drafted this document with the help of the plan which García de la
Cadena was about to proclaim before his arrest in 1886. It certainly possesses
a cosmopolitanism absent from earlier statements of his aims.

The Plan de Conitaca called for a radical redrawing of state boundaries, the
relocation of the federal capital from Mexico to Dolores Hidalgo (in Guanajuato
and symbolic birth place of the Mexican nation), the creation of new states in the

[68] Alicia Hernández Chávez, 'Origen y ocaso del ejército porfiriano', *Historia Mexicana*, Vol. 153,
1989, pp. 271-72.

[69] D. Cosío Villegas, *Historia Moderna de México: El Porfiriato, La Vida Política Interior. Parte
Primera*, pp. 615-23; Charles Hale, *The Transformation of Liberalism*, pp. 58, 67, 105.

Valle de México, Jalisco's canton of Tepic, and the Laguna de Tlahualilo (currently partitioned by the states of Durango, Chihuahua and Coahuila), free exercise of suffrage, the emancipation of the municipalities as the fourth power of the state, abolition of the death penalty, the right of settlements of more than 2,000 to receive municipal status and land, the entitlement to the rank of captain of any person able to raise sixty men in a National Guard unit, etc., followed by various patriotic exhortations.

Among these grander constitutional ideals, Bernal's plan is punctuated by personal justifications for his decision to rebel on behalf of the villages of central and southern Sinaloa which he claimed to represent. One passage merits reproduction here for what it reveals of the deception felt by local leaders who had supported the Liberal cause, but received little (in terms of respect for constitutional guarantees or local liberties) in return:

'Cuando la traición me privó de un jefe y de un amigo en la persona del general Jesús Ramírez Terrón, partidario de los tuxtepecanos…me resigné a vivir aislado, en un pueblo infeliz, aunque con la mira de esperar la oportunidad y la hora para volver al servicio de mi esclavizada patria. Los gobiernos de Durango y Sinaloa se obstinaron en perseguirme, hasta que no pudiendo vivir con garantías en mi hogar, me resolví lanzarme a un terreno harto difícil y peligroso, porque la revolución no tomaba forma decisiva; el país se manifestaba dispuesto pero faltaban caudillos y centro de unión paro todos los partidarios…….Después de cuatro años de privaciones, de miserias y peligros, he logrado dominar en esta Serranía, en mas de treinta leguas a la redonda, sin embargo de que tropas de México, de Durango y Sinaloa, me persiguen y asedian por todas partes….Soy favorecido y mis soldados son dueños de cuanto el favor pone en nuestras manos. Firme en el propósito de hacer el bien, pero sin los tamaños necesarios para encabezar un movimiento popular y dirigirlo, iba a prestar mi escaso contingente a quien debía ser guía de todos nosotros (Trinidad García de la Cadena)…Pero como la fortuna de Tuxtepec y su sed de sangre han puesto de otro modo las cosas, yo me he decidido a seguir las indicaciones de los que todavía viven y están resueltos a llevar las cosas al resultado que nos proponemos….Me importan poco las calificaciones que se hacen de mí. Todos los revolucionarios han sido llamados bandidos, sin embargo, hasta ahora no me he enriquecido yo con los despojos de nadie…'

The timing of Bernal's Plan de Conitaca was not perfect. The elections of 1888 were still more a year away. And, despite his national fame as a bandit, he was not considered in opposition circles as a serious contender for national leadership. Based (most likely) upon García de la Cadena's abortive *pronunciamiento* of 1886, the plan was too ambitious for the band which pronounced it. Heraclio Bernal's firm command over his following and his region of the Sierra de Sinaloa were not in doubt. But this remote *cacicazgo* was inadequate even for making much of an impression upon state politics, let alone upon the national political scene. With federal support, such a movement might have been deemed useful for ousting an unpopular or expendable state governor. But after twelve years of federal army persecution, no such option was available to Bernal in 1887.

The movements in Sinaloa led by Ramírez Terrón and Heraclio Bernal represented a Jacobin provincial tradition favouring political decentralisation, the popular election of *jefes políticos* and municipal presidents, going back to the 1850s, probably even earlier. But to allow such an autonomous *cacicazgo* to prevail, in a territory traversed by the principal commercial and silver route between the north-west central states and the coast, was a risk the federal government was not prepared to take. García de la Cadena's ambition to shift the centre of equilibrium of the federation from the valley of Mexico to the Bajío depended upon access to the Pacific through client *cacicazgos* such as Lozada in Tepic and later Bernal in Sinaloa. This, understandably, was seen in Mexico City as a threat not only to the political order of the states of the north-west central region, but to national territorial integrity. Tepic eventually gained its autonomy as the state of Nayarit. Bernal's dream of an autonomous Sierra de Conitaca, however, came to nothing.[70]

A similar regional movement occured in northern Tamaulipas, during the disordered 1891-2 presidential election. Commanded by Catarino Garza, a journalist of impeccable *tuxtepecano* credentials, this popular rural movement provoked a comparably resolute response from Díaz, once it had become evident that Garza (much as had Trinidad García de la Cadena during the early 1880s) was attracting support from other *tuxtepecano* veterans in the region, such as Gerónimo Treviño and Francisco Naranja in Coahuila, as well as from Díaz's old enemy in Chihuahua, Luis Terrazas.[71]

Elsewhere, such sub-regional movements could command a better relationship with the federal government. In Chihuahua, during the 1870s and 1880s, the western Sierra received the backing of Díaz against the Terrazas clan which controlled the centre of the state.[72] In Coahuila in 1893, the federal government supported the suppression of the *jefes políticos*, because of their use by one of the four main regional factions to dominate the other three. The federal government insisted, however, that one district – the Sierra Mojada – should retain a federally appointed *jefe político*, leaving the federal government

---

[70] Nicole Giron, *Heraclio Bernal ¿Bandolero cacique o precursor de la Revolución?* (Mexico, 1976); and Mario Gill, 'Heraclio Bernal, caudillo frustrado', *Historia Mexicana*, No. 4, 1954, pp.138-58.

[71] José Luis Navarro Burciaga, 'Catarino Garza, periodista opositor a Porfirio Díaz en Tamaulipas', in Friedrich Katz, *Porfirio Díaz Frente al Descontento Popular*, pp. 59-78.

[72] Mark Wasserman, 'Chihuahua. Family Power, Foreign Enterprise and National Control', in Benjamin and McNellie, *Other Mexicos*, p. 41.

a lever in Coahuilan politics, but more importantly, removing an assertive mining district which had threatened to upset the alternation between regional power groups for the control of the state.[73] In the south, particularly in Díaz's home state of Oaxaca and in Guerrero, sub-regional *cacicazgos* could expect federal toleration, even indulgence, providing *caciques* kept to themselves (much as did Fidencio Hernández and Guillermo Meijueiro in the Sierra de Ixtlán) or, should they rebel (as Diego Alvarez did in 1893, without incurring federal disapproval), this should serve the federal objective of restoring equilibrium to the internal politics of the state.[74]

Conclusion

The inflexibility that characterised the response of the central power in Spain to manifestations of local and regional sovereignty contrasts with the far wider variety of options enjoyed by the central power in Mexico, ranging from the granting of autonomy in the formation of a new federal entity, at one extreme of a lengthy continuum, to forceful repression, at the other. Political virtue in Mexico was born of necessity for, throughout much of the century, the central power was too weak to impose any coherent centralising project. In Mexico, from the 1820s, Conservative administrations favoured dismemberment of potentially overmighty colonial provinces, in order to increase the centre's leverage over the states. From the 1850s, with the collapse of the old army, and its replacement by the National Guards of the states, both the federal and state constitutions, drafted in the heat of the war against the Conservatives, at first aspired to guarantee varying degrees of regional and local autonomy and sovereignty. In Spain, by contrast, a strong and centralised army, encouraged by regional oligarchies and sanctioned 'conservative-Liberal' statesmen such as Emilio Castelar, succeeded in crushing cantonalist and federalist movements which had sought smaller provincial units and a greater degree of regional autonomy.

The institution of the *jefe político* made an important contribution to Mexico's constitutional and geo-political flexibility. In Puebla, Sonora, Sinaloa and Campeche (and, doubtless, elsewhere too), the *jefes políticos*, intended initially, when they were established in 1814, as mere agents of the Crown on the local level, became, for short periods, embodiments of district sovereignty. This proved an effective (albeit only temporary) solution to assertive, and potentially disruptive local and regional *cacicazgos*. An additional element of flexibility was the encouragement, by Conservatives and Liberals alike, of a process of

---

[73] Romana Falcón, 'La desaparición de los jefes políticos en Coahuila'; and 'Logros y límites de la centralización porfirista. Coahuila vista desde arriba', in Anne Staples et al, *El dominio de las minorías: república restaurada y porfiriato* (Mexico, 1989), pp. 95-136.

[74] Jaime Salazar Adame, 'Movimientos populares durante el porfiriato en el estado de Guerrero (1885-1891)', in Friedrich Katz, *Porfirio Díaz frente al descontento popular*, pp. 97-121.

fragmentation of Mexico's large historic provinces, inherited from the Colony, into smaller and more manageable entities (an aspiration which was effectively opposed in Spain, where it was thought it might become the first step towards national disintegration). Mexico's constitutional flexibility and habit of boundary gerrymandering was born, it should be repeated, of political and often military necessity. However, once the age of revolution and 'regeneration' gave way to the peace of the Porfiriato, federal and state constitutions rapidly became more centralised, *jefes políticos* returned to become the agents of governors (although with often greater political skill, tact and individual initiative than they have traditionally been credited with), and state boundaries were stabilised, leaving less space for cantonal secessions and adhesions.

With the outbreak of the revolution in 1910, the potential of the *jefe político* to become the embodiment of local sovereignty, and to serve as a buffer between local and central power, once more became evident. The popular elections of *jefes políticos* in the state of Guanajuato in 1911 offered a route out of riot and political crisis.[75] However, because of the poor image of the *jefe político* as the oppressive agent of political centralisation under the *ancien régime*, the office became an obvious target for a young revolutionary state aspiring to enhance its popularity as well as to increase its direct control at the local level. In 1914, the *jefes políticos* were finally abolished by Venustiano Carranza as symbols of repression.[76] What more convenient oversimplification of their historical role by a state determined finally to erase the gap between central and local power?

---

[75] Mónica Blanco, 'Participación Popular y Revolución. La elección de los jefes políticos en Guanajuato en 1911', in *Memoria del Congreso Internacional sobre la Revolución Mexicana* (Mexico, 1991), Vol. II, pp.135-47.

[76] J. Lloyd Mecham, 'The Jefe Político in Mexico', p.351.

CHAPTER 3

Representación de Europa y discurso nacionalista en los relatos de viajes colombianos, 1850-1900

Frédéric Martinez

El viaje a Europa en la Colombia del siglo XIX, y la creación de una literatura nacional.

Al emprender el estudio de las representaciones de las naciones europeas en Colombia en el siglo XIX, de su producción y de su difusión, siente uno su mirada más atraída hacia la actividad de las élites nacionales que leen, viajan, escriben, hacen negocios y gobiernan, que hacia el estudio de los intereses económicos y diplomáticos de las potencias europeas o el de los pocos grupos de inmigrantes europeos que van a buscar en esta lejana tierra un destino más envidiable.[1] La presencia europea en Colombia, débil en comparación con otras naciones hispanoamericanas, parece jugar efectivamente un papel muy secundario en la difusión de un discurso sobre Europa, comparada con la inmensa atracción ejercida entre las élites nacionales por el viejo continente.

Durante la primera mitad del siglo XIX, las familias patricias de la Nueva Granada van demostrando un interés cada vez mayor hacia el viaje a Europa, que comienza a aparecer como el complemento de una buena educación criolla. Sin embargo los viajes de Francisco de P. Santander, de Ezequiel Rojas, de Joaquín Acosta o de Florentino González, a pesar del interés que despiertan en la sociedad granadina, no dejan de ser excepciones. A mediados de siglo, con la introducción del vapor en la navegación transatlántica, empieza a afirmarse más claramente el apego de las élites colombianas al viaje a Europa: más allá de algunas expatriaciones más o menos voluntarias, un número cada vez mayor de colombianos acomodados se embarcan rumbo al viejo mundo para encargarse de un puesto diplomático, para desarrollar sus negocios de exportación e importación, para completar su educación o para hacer una peregrinación a la Tierra Santa (y frecuentemente por todas estas razones reunidas). Este flujo de viajeros de un lado y otro del atlántico, nuevo en su importancia, engendra una significativa producción de representaciones de las naciones europeas, en una medida que nunca antes se había experimentado en Colombia.

---

[1] Durante el período estudiado, la actual república de Colombia lleva sucesivamente los nombres de República de Nueva Granada, Confederación Neo-Granadina, Estados Unidos de Colombia, y República de Colombia. Para mayor comodidad, utilizaremos indistintamente los términos 'Colombia' y 'colombiano'.

En las páginas de los periódicos colombianos los viajeros publican 'revistas' y 'correspondencias', en las que cuentan sus experiencias en las capitales europeas y escriben sus consideraciones acerca de las instituciones políticas, sociales, religiosas, económicas y culturales de los principales países del viejo mundo que van recorriendo. Las traducciones de artículos extraídos de la prensa europea, las reproducciones de artículos que publican en español los publicistas hispanoamericanos que residen en París o en Londres se multiplican. En los periódicos, en fin, se escribe la crónica de las llegadas y salidas de los colombianos que viajan a Europa. Numerosos literatos y estadistas dedican algunos capítulos de sus memorias a su o sus estadía(s) en Europa.[2] Un nuevo género literario se desarrolla así en las incipientes letras colombianas a partir de mediados de siglo: el relato de viaje.

Entre 1847 y 1893 se publican 17 relatos de viaje a Europa o a la Tierra Santa (lo que contrasta con el escaso número de relaciones de viajes a Estados Unidos que se publican en el mismo período), a los que se agregan todos los textos publicados por entrega en los periódicos y las revistas.[3] Varios políticos de primer orden suscriben a esta moda literaria.[4] Entre los liberales, José María Samper (1862), Ramón Gómez (1880), Felipe Pérez (1882), Medardo Rivas (1885), son los más prominentes. Entre los conservadores se destacan eminentes políticos y publicistas como Alberto Urdaneta (1879) o Carlos Holguín (1880-1881) y varios clérigos – el obispo de Pasto, Manuel Canuto Restrepo (1871), el jesuita Federico Cornelio Aguilar(1875), el misionero José Santiago de la Peña (1860), o el seminarista Domingo Arosemena (1859) – quienes publican la relación de su peregrinación a la Tierra Santa.

Como consecuencia de esta generalización del viaje a Europa entre las élites granadinas surge la emergencia de una literatura nacional sobre Europa, que corresponde a una voluntad de las élites colombianas de apropriarse del discurso sobre las naciones del viejo mundo. Liberales y conservadores promueven explícitamente las razones por las que buscan 'nacionalizar' la visión de Europa en su patria. Para los conservadores, la lucha contra la amenaza que representa la difusión de las ideas impías venidas de ultramar justifica la publicación de textos sobre Europa purgados de todo riesgo de contaminación irreligiosa. José

---

[2]   Ver José Hilario López, *Memorias* (1857) (Medellín, 1969); José María Samper, *Historia de una alma* (1881) (Bogotá, 1948); Aníbal Galindo, *Recuerdos Históricos* (Bogotá, 1900); Aquileo Parra, *Memorias* (Bogotá, 1912); y José María Quijano Wallis, *Memorias autobiográficas, histórico-políticas y de carácter social* (Grattoferrata, 1919).

[3]   Ver Gabriel Giraldo Jaramillo, *Bibliografía colombiana de viajes* (Bogotá, 1957) y José de Onis, *The United States as seen by Spanish American writers, 1776-1890* (New York, 1975).

[4]   Ver, por ejemplo, José María Samper, *Viajes de un colombiano a Europa*, 2 vols. (París, 1862); Felipe Pérez, *Episodios de un viaje* (1882) (Bogotá, 1946); Alberto Urdaneta, 'Una excursión a España', en *El Repertorio Colombiano*, Bogotá, diciembre 1879, pp 457-64; enero 1880, pp. 20-8; marzo 1880, pp. 161-3; Carlos Holguín, 'Revista de Francia', *El Repertorio Colombiano*, Bogotá, enero de 1881, pp. 74-88; 'Revista de Europa', *El Repertorio Colombiano*, Bogotá, diciembre de 1881, pp. 427-53.

Santiago de la Peña, un misionero colombiano que publica en 1860 sus 'Noticias de Jerusalén', reconoce su afición a los relatos de viajes a Palestina que se publican en Europa, pero recomienda la mayor prudencia en su lectura :

'El venir a la Palestina a visitar los Santos Lugares de nuestra redención lo considero como una cosa necesaria a todo cristiano, pues no es lo mismo leer las relaciones de los viajeros i peregrinos, porque todo cuanto puedan decir estos es nada, i no puede formarse idea de lo que es en realidad: cada uno cuenta las cosas que ha visto, según como las concibe, i según como esté su corazón desposeído de las ideas que infunde la relijión.'[5]

Embarcándose en Marsella para el Oriente en 1858, de la Peña descubre con espanto el nacimiento del turismo europeo a Palestina y se indigna frente al espectáculo de la extraña mezcla de la piedad con el divertimiento en las caravanas europeas.[6] Con el propósito de prevenir cualquier riesgo de contaminación irreligiosa que amenace a los peregrinos americanos, de la Peña aboga por la organización de una caravana hispanoamericana a Palestina a cargo del clero granadino. En su libro *Sensaciones en Oriente*, que publica en Nueva York en 1859, Domingo Arosemena explica que su mayor propósito al dar esta obra a la imprenta es el de colmar la ausencia de escritos nacionales sobre los Lugares Santos que observa en su patria. Otros países hispanoamericanos, como Chile, Perú o México ya dieron a luz una literatura propia sobre el tema. Arosemena explica entonces que su obra no ofrece nada nuevo, sino un texto redactado en un 'lenguaje nacional', relatando con sinceridad las cosas que ha visto por sí mismo.[7]

Así, a partir de la publicación en 1847 de las cartas del joven M.I. Cordóvez Moure – quien había sido el primer granadino en viajar a Palestina en 1845 (publicación que justifica el editor por el hecho de ser la obra de 'un hijo de nuestras selvas, sin los viejos hábitos, sin las exageradas pretensiones ni el fatal escepticismo del europeo'[8] – hasta los homenajes tributados por José Caicedo Rojas y José Maria Torres Caicedo[9] al loable deseo de los colombianos de viajar a Oriente y de difundir a sus compatriotas las luces de la verdadera religión, gracias a la crónica de sus peregrinaciones, se va esbozando un cuerpo de literatura nacional acerca de la Tierra Santa.

---

[5]   José Santiago de la Peña, *Noticias de Jerusalén* (Bogotá, 1860), pp. 55-6.

[6]   *Ibid.*, p. 73

[7]   Domingo Arosemena, *Sensaciones en oriente o impresiones bíblicas de un granadino en la Tierra Santa* (New York, 1859), p. V.

[8]   Manuel Ignacio Cordóvez Moure, *La primera visita de un granadino a la Tierra Santa* (Bogotá, 1847), p. 2.

[9]   José Caicedo Rojas, Introducción a Rafael Duque Uribe, *Recuerdos de la Tierra Santa* (Bogotá, 1869), p. XX, y José María Torres Caicedo, Introducción a Nicolás Pardo, *Impresiones de viaje de Italia a la Palestina y Egipto* (París, 1872).

Los viajeros liberales elaboran también un discurso de pedagogía nacional para justificar sus publicaciones. En 1862, José María Samper se queja de que los únicos escritos sobre Europa que se han difundido en Colombia han sido novelas como las de Alejandro Dumas y muchos otros escritores franceses 'que desnaturalizan las cosas a fuerza de ingenio, exageración o fantasía, y prescinden de los hechos sociales, ocupándose solo de lo pintoresco y divertido'[10] o estudios especializados incomprensibles para la mayoría de los lectores. Samper se propone colmar ese vacío con una gran síntesis pedagógica sobre Europa escrita para el lector colombiano, que empieza entonces a publicar en París: los *Viajes de un colombiano a Europa*.

La guerra de las representaciones de Europa

La inevitable consecuencia de la voluntad de las élites colombianas de 'nacionalizar' el discurso sobre Europa es el aumento de su densidad polémica: al introducir una perspectiva nacional, los viajeros reflejan la polarización del debate político y luego polarizan a su vez la representación del viejo continente. Liberales y conservadores, que se oponen de manera crónica en los aspectos político, ideológico y militar, durante la segunda mitad del siglo XIX, encuentran un nuevo campo de batalla cuando se ponen a retratar las naciones de Europa occidental que ambos consideran como la máxima expresión de la civilización. Los periódicos, la literatura política, y los relatos de viaje nos permiten reconstituir los rasgos esenciales de las dos principales representaciones que compiten en el debate político colombiano: la Europa de los conservadores y la Europa de los liberales.

La representación liberal de Europa encuentra sin lugar a dudas su máxima expresión en los textos que José María Samper escribe en París al comienzo de los años 1860: *Viajes de un colombiano a Europa* (1862), *Cartas de un Americano* publicadas en el periódico limeño *El Comercio* (1862) y el clásico *Ensayo sobre las revoluciones políticas* (1861). Con esos escritos, Samper se impone como el principal defensor e ideólogo del discurso liberal sobre Europa en el debate político colombiano. Al abogar, en el *Ensayo*, por la destrucción de las instituciones coloniales en su patria, Samper retrata en su relato de viajes una Europa desgarrada por la guerra en que el liberalismo está empeñado para derrumbar el antiguo régimen. Esa representación, haciendo eco a la pugna del liberalismo americano contra los vestigios de la colonia, adquiere en su obra un fuerte valor paradigmático. Samper esquematiza su percepción para volverla aún más ejemplar para el lector liberal a quien se dirige, y propone una 'cartografía' liberal de Europa, marcando las ciudades que visita con signos positivos (liberalismo, tolerancia religiosa, cosmopolitanismo, industria, luz) o negativos (absolutismo, clericalismo, inmovilismo, desaseo, mendicidad, oscuridad). Así

---

[10] Samper, *Viajes de un colombiano a Europa*, Vol. 2, p. 3.

va retratando, de un lado, la Europa liberal y moderna – simbolizada por Londres, Losana, Barcelona, Marsella, Bordeus, Bruselas – y del otro, la vieja Europa, aristócratica, clerical y absolutista - Toledo, Brujas, Malinas, Lovaina, Karlsruhe, Friburgo.

Al hojear los relatos de viajes de Samper, Rivas, Pérez, Pereira Gamba, Pardo, Parra y Quijano Wallis, se van reconstituyendo los principales tópicos de la representación liberal de Europa: el homenaje a la herencia de la revolución francesa, al nacimiento de la tercera república, a la unificación italiana y al régimen de Víctor Manuel, la evocación de la libertad religiosa en Suiza y Alemania, los elogios a las prisiones y los establecimientos correccionales de Europa y la crítica del despotismo de Napoleón III. Para completar el cuadro, cabe anotar que, con excepción del liberal Nicolás Pardo, cónsul de Colombia en Italia a comienzos de la década del setenta, los liberales no viajan a Palestina. El viaje a Oriente es decididamente un monopolio conservador.

La representación conservadora de Europa ofrece un retrato invertido: los conservadores denuncian la influencia del protestantismo y los progresos de la impiedad, la nefanda influencia de los filósofos y de la revolución francesa, la corrupción de la juventud, la política anticlerical de los gobiernos europeos (la España liberal, la Italia de Víctor Manuel, la Tercera República Francesa). En oposición a la Europa ideal de los liberales, los conservadores pintan una Europa católica, y ensalzan su capacidad de reacción contra los ataques anticlericales. En 1869 el antioqueño Andrés Posada evoca así la sobrevivencia de la Francia católica :

'La patria de San Luis no ha apostatado por entero; aun se cantan en sus templos las alabanzas del Altísimo, se lleva la ofrenda a sus altares, se enjugan las lágrimas del desgraciado i se busca en el santuario de la penitencia la paz y el perdón. La cátedra sagrada no ha enmudecido todavía: los Bossuet, los Massillon, tienen aún sus sucesores; la fe cuenta adalides como Gaume y Augusto Nicolás.' [11]

El discurso conservador evoca los oradores sagrados franceses,[12] las instituciones ejemplares del catolicismo europeo como la Obra de Propaganda de la Fe, fundada en Lyon en 1822,[13] la grandeza de la Iglesia galicana y de sus

---

[11] Andrés Posada Arango, *Viaje de América a Jerusalén, tocando en París, Londres, Loreto, Roma i Ejipto* (París, 1869), p. 35.

[12] Posada Arango, *Viaje de América a Jerusalén*, p. 35; y Arosemena, *Sensaciones de oriente*, p. 4.

[13] Arosemena, *Sensaciones de oriente*, pp. 3-5.

prelados Dupanloup y Sibour.[14] La geografía conservadora del antiguo mundo es esencialmente una geografía piadosa que incluye Roma, Lourdes, Loreto, Palestina y Lyon, ciudad distinguida por el catolicismo ferviente de su pueblo.[15] Si el discurso liberal destaca el papel civilizador que desempeñan los países de Europa a través de la difusión del liberalismo, los conservadores exaltan el papel civilizador de la empresa evangélica llevada a cabo por los países de la Europa católica en el Medio Oriente contra Mahoma y la Iglesia rusa, en el Extremo Oriente contra el paganismo y el protestantismo inglés, y describen a Napoleón III como un monarca católico. La presencia occidental en Oriente proporciona una serie de íconos ejemplares: la piedad de los misioneros de Tierra Santa, la resistencia de los clérigos perseguidos por los gobiernos anticlericales de Europa, la obra civilizadora del cristianismo.

La densidad polémica del discurso sobre Europa, que entraña ese desdoblamiento de su representación, revela que Europa se ha convertido en un terreno de discordia en la lucha que opone a conservadores y liberales. La moda literaria del viaje a Oriente ofrece una buena ilustración de este fenómeno. El auge del relato de viaje a Oriente corresponde precisamente al período de predominio liberal en el poder (de 1849 a 1878, con el paréntesis del gobierno conservador de Mariano Ospina de 1857 a 1861) que causa la separación de la Iglesia y del Estado, la expulsión de los jesuitas, la desamortización de los bienes de manos muertas, y la casi aniquilación de las órdenes religiosas regulares. Entre 1847 y 1875 se publican diez relatos de viajes a Oriente. Durante estos años, la Iglesia colombiana anima a los viajeros a que publiquen los relatos de sus peregrinaciones a la Tierra Santa, con el fin de oponer una propaganda religiosa al movimiento de laicización de la enseñanza y de la sociedad que promueven los gobiernos liberales.

En 1856, el editor de *El Catolicismo*, al publicar una carta de Domingo Arosemena, quien realiza entonces un viaje a Palestina, anota: 'Esperamos que el señor Arosemena, a ejemplo de Chateaubriand i del Abad Geramb, estimule a la juventud contemporánea con la relación circunstanciada de su viaje e impresiones que recibió al estudio de la sagrada (…) i a la visita provechosa de los Santos Lugares que la recuerden'.[16] En la introducción a *Sensaciones en Oriente*, que publica en Nueva York tres años más tarde, Arosemena recuerda que fue al leer esta exhortación del clero a la difusión de las luces de la religión católica cuando formó el proyecto de un libro para sus conciudadanos. En 1869, el obispo de Medellín aconseja a Monseñor Restrepo la publicación del relato de su viaje a Oriente: 'Déme Ud ese gusto, pues que esa clase de publicaciones

---

[14] Posada Arango, *Viaje de América a Jerusalén*, p. 31, y Arosemena, *Sensaciones de oriente*, p. 370.

[15] Posada Arango, *Viaje de América a Jerusalén*, p. 256, y Arosemena, *Sensaciones de oriente*, pp. 3-5.

[16] *El Catolicismo*, 5 febrero 1856.

aprovechan mucho al pueblo cristiano, y con especialidad al de Antioquia, tan distinguido por su piedad'.[17]

La convicción de que la publicación de un viaje a Palestina es un acto militante de defensa del clero colombiano llega a ser general: en 1870, el editor del periódico *La Caridad* comenta así la partida de dos clérigos para los Santos Lugares: 'Deseándoles feliz viaje y próspera vuelta, celebramos su proyecto que no puede menos de redundar en pro de la Iglesia por los nuevos conocimientos que adquirirán los peregrinos viajeros visitando los lugares donde tuvo lugar nuestra redención, y las cultas ciudades de Europa'.[18] Sin embargo, con la década del setenta se acaba la densidad política que los relatos de viajes a la Tierra Santa habían adquirido desde el comienzo de los años cincuenta. La elección de Rafael Núñez a la presidencia anuncia la destruccion del dispositivo anticlerical del Estado liberal. Con el Concordato de 1887, la Iglesia vuelve a recobrar el poder económico, social y educativo que los gobiernos radicales le habían negado. La producción de relatos de viajes a Oriente ya no tiene utilidad: después de la publicación de 'Recuerdos de un viaje a Oriente' del jesuita Aguilar, en 1875, va desapareciendo este género literario por varias décadas.

Mientras que los conservadores exaltan la difusión de las luces de la religión desde el viejo mundo, los liberales explican su voluntad pedagógica de luchar contra el atraso de la sociedad colombiana por la difusión de obras de vulgarizacion sobre la civilizacion moderna venida de ultramar. En 1862, José María Samper escribe:

'Viajo por mi patria, es decir con el solo fin de serle útil, y escribo para mis compatriotas los Hispano-colombianos. He creído que lo que importa más por el momento no es profundizar ciertos estudios, sino vulgarizar o generalizar nociones. A los pueblos de Hispano-colombia no les ha llegado todavía el momento de los estudios fuertes, por la sencilla razón de que la inmensa masa popular no tiene aún la noción general del progreso europeo. Hasta tanto que esa masa no haya recibido la infusión elemental de luz y fuerza que necesita para emprender su marcha (porque hoy no se marcha sino que se anda a tientas) el mejor servicio que se le pueda hacer es el de la simple vulgarización de las ideas elementales. Después vendrá el tiempo de los trabajos laboriosos y profundos.

La inmensa mayoría de los Hispano-colombianos no conoce, por falta de contacto íntimo con Europa, los rudimentos o las verdaderas condiciones del juego general de la política, las letras, la industria, el comercio, y todos los grandes intereses vinculados en Europa. De ahí provienen graves errores de apreciación, de imitación o de indiferencia que se revelan en la

---

[17] Manuel Canuto Restrepo, *Viaje a Roma y Jerusalén* (París, 1871).

[18] *La Caridad*, 16 julio 1870.

política, la literatura, la legislación y las manifestaciones económicas de Hispano-Colombia.

Desvanecer, si puedo, esos errores, dándole a la expresión de lo que me parece la verdad las formas simpáticas de lo pintoresco y el atractivo de una rápida, fiel y animada narración, tal es el objeto de estas páginas de impresiones.'[19]

El estudio de estas representaciones contrarias, si bien demuestra el carácter polémico que adquiere la referencia a Europa en el debate político colombiano, tiene también la ventaja de revelar el consenso que existe acerca del valor ejemplar de la política europea. Todos reconocen implícitamente que el debate sobre la evolución política de las naciones de Europa occidental es pertinente y útil al debate político colombiano.[20] Positivamente, liberales y conservadores construyen un discurso pedagógico sobre las instituciones modelos nacidas en el Viejo Mundo: el liberalismo y la tolerancia religiosa para los primeros, la caridad, las órdenes misioneras y la resistencia del clero para los segundos. Negativamente, ellos denuncian la amenaza europea: la impiedad o la disgregación social para los conservadores, el poder aristocrático, la tiranía o el clericalismo para los liberales. Las naciones europeas aparecen indudablemente como fuentes de referencias políticas múltiples.[21]

Más allá del carácter ejemplar que todos reconocen a la política europea, por ir todos a buscar en ella los modelos que les convienen,[22] aparecen otros puntos comunes entre liberales y conservadores, que tienden a acreditar la idea de que existen más puntos de convergencia que de divergencia entre ellos respecto a su

---

[19] Samper, *Viajes de un colombiano*, pp. 2-3.

[20] Es interesante observar la diferencia de densidad polémica entre los distintos países europeos que 'cuentan' en los debates políticos de Colombia. De manera general, el discurso sobre los países que conocen conflictos comparables a los que dividen las élites colombianas es claramente polémico (así ocurre con Francia, Italia y España, en particular en lo que atañe a las relaciones entre Iglesia y Estado) mientras que la representación de naciones que tienen instituciones que son mas difícilmente comparables tiende a ser más consensual entre los colombianos. En el caso de Francia e Italia en particular, se oponen muy explícitamente las representaciones liberales y conservadoras. No se puede decir lo mismo del discurso sobre Inglaterra, en el que los puntos de vistas liberales y conservadores apenas se diferencian: todos exaltan el parlamentarismo, las libertades individuales, lamentan la miseria urbana y admiran el progreso industrial. Apenas se puede advertir una diferencia en la crítica que hacen los liberales a Inglaterra por ser la 'tierra clásica' de la aristocracia.

[21] José Carlos Mariátegui comenta así la ambivalencia de la referencia francesa en el debate sobre la educación en el Perú en el siglo XIX: 'La influencia francesa se insertó más tarde en este cuadro, con la complacencia así de quienes miraban en Francia la patria de la libertad jacobina y republicana como de quienes se inspiraban en el pensamiento y la práctica de la restauración'. José Carlos Mariátegui, *Siete ensayos de interpretación de la realidad peruana* (México, 1979), p. 144.

[22] Malcolm Deas, en su estudio sobre la influencia inglesa en Colombia, considera que el eclecticismo en la referencia europea es una característica de la cultura criolla: 'El eclecticismo, el hábito de escoger lo que convenga en cualquier parte, me parece us rasgo que se encuentra muy temprano en la cultura criolla, y muy persistente'. M. Deas, 'La influencia inglesa – y otras influencias – en Colombia, 1880-1930', *Nueva Historia de Colombia*, Vol. 3 (Bogotá, 1989).

percepción de Europa. Todos demuestran un gran interés por los logros del progreso material (hoteles, ferrocarriles y buques de vapor merecen un lugar muy especial en sus libros), al mismo tiempo que se preocupan por la evolución de la sociedad europea y por los peligros sociales que perciben en ella. Si algunos de los vicios de las sociedades europeas dan lugar a un discurso polémico (la impiedad que denuncian los conservadores, el aristocratismo que critican los liberales) liberales y conservadores están generalmente de acuerdo respecto de las peligros sociales que amenazan a Europa: la miseria, los vicios, la corrupción, la prostitución, la disolución de los lazos famliares y sociales, la ausencia de control social, el anonimato, el suicidio, el socialismo. Una asombrosa unanimidad aparece en la evocación de la Comuna de París: este episodio cristaliza todo el horror de las élites colombianas frente a la amenaza de las 'clases peligrosas'.

Otro punto de convergencia entre los viajeros liberales y conservadores es su tendencia común a describirse a sí mismos en el entorno moderno y civilizado de las capitales europeas. Al mismo tiempo que una mirada a las 'ciudades cultas' de Europa, los viajeros proponen una mirada a sí mismos, y sus relatos ofrecen el autorretrato de una élite ilustrada, distinguida por su acceso momentáneo a las grandes capitales del mundo civilizado.[23]

El debate sobre el viaje: nacionalismo y extranjerismo

Este consenso sobre la utilidad del viaje y la ejemplaridad de Europa llega a ser cuestionado periódicamente durante el siglo XIX, por un debate político e intelectual que denuncia el extranjerismo de los promotores de la civilización europea. Al criticar a inadaptación de la experiencia adquirida en Europa a la situación nacional, los detractores de la moda del viaje le niegan toda utilidad. Los viajeros mismos llaman la atención de los padres de familia sobre los riesgos que amenazan a los hijos que sus padres mandan a estudiar a Europa. Los conservadores, por atraídos que estén por la perspectiva de evitar a sus hijos los estragos de la enseñanza sensualista que promueven los gobiernos liberales en Colombia,[24] temen la contaminación de la impiedad a la que los podrían exponer mandándolos a Europa. 'Yo no mandaría por mi cuenta ningún joven

---

[23] David Viñas, en su estudio sobre los relatos de viajes argentinos del siglo XIX, subraya el papel de distinción social que cumple el discurso sobre Europa: 'Es así como Europa a partir de Caseros y en especial luego de 1880 a través del grupo social que detenta la literatura, se convierte en proyección y ratificación de las distancias sociales: es decir Europa exalta y sacraliza las distancias sociales instauradas en América'; David Viñas, *Literatura argentina y realidad política* (Buenos Aires, 1946), p. 46.

[24] Frank Safford, *El ideal de lo práctico*, capítulo 6, 'Los estudios en el exterior' (Bogotá, 1989), pp. 221-52.

a educarse en París a no ser en el seminario de San Sulpicio o en los colegios dirijidos por los jesuitas', anota Monseñor Restrepo en 1871.[25]

Los liberales, espantados por la corrupción de las costumbres que reina en las capitales europeas, y en París en particular, demuestran la misma desconfianza respecto de los estudios en Europa. Felipe Pérez se burla de la ingenuidad de los padres que creen que los estudios en París son benéficos para sus hijos.[26] Y Medardo Rivas, cuyos dos hijos estudiaron varios años en un colegio londinense, recomienda a los padres de familia colombianos una solución más adecuada:

'Y a propósito de este vivo deseo, me atrevo a dar un consejo a los hombres acomodados de Colombia, y especialmente a los de nuestras tierras cálidas, que, deseosos de educar a sus hijos, los envían a Alemania a que mueran tísicos, a Francia a corromperse o a Inglaterra a inutilizarse, y es el de que en vez de mandarlos a iniciarse en los misterios de una civilización que ningún punto de contacto tiene con la de las tierras cálidas de nuestro país y de la cual por mucho que aprendan, nada pueden aplicar, los envíen a Jamaica...'[27]

En un artículo que lleva el título de 'Nostalgia en la patria', publicado en la revista conservadora *El Repertorio Colombiano* en 1879, Carlos Eduardo Coronado explica que la moda del viaje a ultramar revela un vicio más profundo que envenena las costumbres de las clases acomodadas de Colombia: la idolatría por lo extranjero y el desprecio hacia lo nacional. Este vicio, debido en buena parte al desarrollo de las relaciones comerciales con Europa y América del Norte, se difunde con la moda de los relatos de viajes que dan de estos lejanos países una falsa imagen. Los colombianos que viajan a Europa por su propio placer no sacan ninguna ventaja de esa experiencia: demasiado rápido, sin meta precisa, el viaje turístico no les permite ni aprender mucho de las sociedades que atraviesan, ni siquiera familiarizarse con sus idiomas. Al contrario, la experiencia superficial que es para la mayoría de los viajeros una estadía en Europa les da la ilusión de una vida distinta – 'En los hoteles se siente uno tratado como un príncipe, y por fin acaba por creer que lo es', anota Coronado[28] – y se convierten, una vez de vuelta en la patria, en unos inadaptados que gastan su fortuna en la importación de bienes de lujo. Coronado le niega al viaje a Europa, así como al relato de viaje, todo valor pedagógico: 'Con mucha desconfianza debe, pues, recibirse lo que los touristes nos traigan como estudios

---

[25] Restrepo, *Viaje a Roma*, p. 49.

[26] Pérez, *Episodios de un viaje*, p. 176.

[27] Medardo Rivas, *Viajes por Colombia, Francia, Inglaterra y Alemania* (Bogotá, 1885), p. 136.

[28] Carlos Eduardo Coronado, 'Nostalgia en la patria', *El Repertorio Colombiano*, Bogotá, septiembre 1879, p. 218.

morales, pescados a la ligera en ferrocarriles, museos, teatros y hoteles, y hechos con las desventajas consiguientes.'[29]

Si los detractores de la referencia europea, al retratar a los colombianos como 'extranjerizantes', construyen un discurso que muestra muchos rasgos de 'costumbrismo',[30] también proponen una crítica más fundamental respecto al carácter ejemplar que los viajeros reconocen a Europa con el fin de valorar su propio viaje como una experiencia que les da más madurez, más ilustración, más civilización. 'En resumen, no negamos que esto constituya una gran ciencia; pero no creemos que haya necesidad de ir a pescarla tan lejos, ni que eso autorice a sus afortunados poseedores para desempeñar a su vuelta a la patria el papel de reformadores de las costumbres'.[31] Efectivamente toda la argumentación que los viajeros elaboran para valorar su estadía en Europa se basa en el postulado que Europa confiere autoridad, una experiencia necesaria a todo colombiano que quiera dedicarse al bién público. José María Samper ofrece uno de los más explícitos ejemplos de utilización de una experiencia europea en una estrategia personal. En las páginas consagradas al relato de su permanencia en Europa en su libro de recuerdos *Historia de una alma*, en 1881 (que es una reescritura puesto que ya había publicado dos tomos de viajes en 1862), Samper dedica numerosas páginas a explicar cómo los años pasados en Europa (entre 1858 y 1862) le han permitido acceder a la madurez política. Alejado del espíritu partidario propio de la política nacional, dedicándose a viajar y a estudiar los principales países europeos, Samper siente la progresiva desaparición de su intransigencia liberal, de su intolerancia ideológica. La familiaridad con algunos colombianos conservadores en París (José María Torres Caicedo, Juan de Francisco Martín) es otro factor que lo lleva a reconsiderar sus opciones políticas y en particular a cuestionar el radicalismo liberal de su juventud. 'El hombre esencialmente americano comenzaba a ceder el paso, en mi ser moral, cuando ya casi se despedía de la primera juventud, al hombre cosmopolita, modificado por las enseñanzas del Viejo Mundo, que comenzaba a entrar en la madurez de sus impresiones y pensamientos.'[32]

Así, gracias a la benéfica influencia de su estadía en Europa, Samper adquiere la convicción de que el patriotismo debe reemplazar al espíritu partidario. Durante una discusión entre liberales colombianos y franceses en el Café Mazarin en París, Samper defiende al presidente conservador Mariano Ospina contra las acusaciones de traidor a la causa federal que le hacen sus copartidarios, apoyados por los franceses, causando así el estupor general.

---

[29] *Ibid.*, p. 216.

[30] La burla de los 'extranjerizantes' y de los hispanoamericanos que se otorgan falsos títulos nobiliarios para lucirse en la buena sociedad de las capitales europeas es un tópico de la literatura sobre Europa; ver Pérez, *Episodios de un viaje*, pp. 186-7; y Rivas, *Viajes por Colombia*, pp. 250-1.

[31] Coronado, *Nostalgia en la patria*, p. 217.

[32] Samper, *Historia de una alma*, p. 266.

Samper se explica entonces con énfasis: 'Aquí soy neo-granadino más que liberal. Aquí no tengo bandera de partido sino la bandera nacional de mi patria, y no consiento en que delante de mí y de ciudadanos que no son compatriotas, se insulte al presidente de mi país.'[33]

El tema del sentimiento patriótico en el extranjero merece un estudio detenido. Es incontestable que el concepto de un engrandecimiento del patriotismo por el viaje al exterior es un tópico del relato de viaje, y eso explica que el viaje merece uno o varios capítulos cuando los hombres públicos escriben sus memorias para dar testimonio a la posteridad de su empeño en la búsqueda del progreso de su patria querida. Al relatar su encuentro con Lesseps que le permite dar noticias a sus compatriotas de la suscripción por el canal interoceánico, Carlos Holguín evoca desde París, en noviembre de 1881, su inquietud por el éxito del proyecto: 'Porque una de las cosas que no sabemos allá es cómo se desarrolla en nosotros por acá el amor por aquel pedazo de tierra infortunada que se llama la patria ausente; y mientras más pequeña y desgraciada la vemos, más nos interesamos por ella.'[34]

Así, dicen los viajeros, unos meses en Europa ofrecen al ciudadano colombiano numerosas oportunidades de fortalecer su sentimiento patriótico y su actitud nacionalista. Cuando se enfrenta con la ignorancia y los prejuicios de los europeos respecto de la América del Sur, el viajero se transforma en entusiasta promotor del estado de civilización de que gozan las naciones latinas. Cuando descubre las iniquidades y los vicios de las sociedades europeas, toma conciencia de la superioridad de las instituciones republicanas, de la libertad de prensa, de la ausencia de una aristocracia en la patria americana. 'Cuando sale uno de las selvas de América y se ve libre de los odios y rencores en que allí se vive, es cuando siente orgullo en ver levantarse a Colombia grande por sus instituciones y presentarse con dignidad entre las naciones más adelantadas del mundo, por haber acabado con la esclavitud y abolido la pena de muerte', escribe Medardo Rivas en 1885.[35]

Entre las manifestaciones de patriotismo de los viajeros, cabe destacar la oración por la patria, como lo hace en 1858 el misionero José Santiago de la Peña, cuando reza en Jerusalén por el porvenir de las repúblicas americanas,[36] la celebración del 20 de julio con la colonia colombiana[37] y la actividad periodística y editorial con el fin de dar a conocer la patria en la prensa y en los círculos intelectuales del viejo mundo. El viajero tiende a retratarse como un

---

[33] *Ibid.*, p. 175.

[34] Holguín, 'Revista de Francia', pp. 86-7.

[35] Rivas, *Viajes por Colombia*, p. 173.

[36] De la Peña, *Noticias de Jerusalén*, pp. 41 y 49.

[37] Nicolás Pardo, *Recuerdos de un viaje a Europa* (Bogotá, 1873), pp. 240-4 y Quijano Wallis, *Memorias autobiográficas*, pp. 380-5.

embajador permanente, preocupado por la sola defensa de su patria en el rango de las naciones civilizadas, guiado en todos sus actos por la trascendencia patriótica. Samper y Torres Caicedo proponen a Lamartine que escriba una biografía de Bolívar; Juan De Francisco Martín y José Joaquín Triana se encargan de la presencia de Colombia en las exposiciones universales; Adriano Paez, Ricardo Pereira y Alberto Urdaneta publican revistas en París:[38] el retrato de la élite colombiana en Europa muestra una clase dirigente totalmente empeñada en extender la fama y el brillo de su lejana e ignorada patria colombiana.

El discurso sobre la densidad patriótica del viaje a Europa tiene entonces varios aspectos: en primer lugar los viajeros defienden su patriotismo 'hacia adentro' que consiste en difundir hacia el pueblo colombiano las luces de la civilización, en su versión liberal o conservadora. En segundo lugar exaltan la labor patriótica que realizan 'hacia afuera', cuando promueven, en la escena de las naciones, la imagen de una Colombia ilustrada, civilizada, adelantada en la vía del progreso. En fin, obran por la patria al transformarse ellos mismos en hombres experimentados, maduros, calificados por su estadía en Europa y luego aptos a dirigir los destinos de la nación colombiana.

El discurso sobre Europa y la lucha por la legitimidad

La existencia de un debate sobre la pertinencia y la utilidad del viaje no debe en nuestro concepto engañarnos acerca de una supuesta división de las élites colombianas entre un grupo cosmopolita y europeizante de un lado y un grupo nacionalista y opuesto a toda influencia extranjera de otro. Liberales y conservadores, capitalinos y provincianos, clérigos y comerciantes, literatos y terratenientes, todos viajan a Europa. En numerosos casos son los mismos viajeros que critican el viaje a Europa, en aparente contradicción con sus actos: Medardo Rivas, al mismo tiempo que exalta la educación inglesa que recibieron sus hijos, busca convencer a los padres colombianos de tierra caliente a que no manden a sus hijos 'a Inglaterra a inutilizarse'. Pedro María Moure, un payanés instalado en Francia en 1839, amigo de Luis Napoleón y prototipo del colombiano aclimatado en el París del Segundo Imperio, critica vehementemente, en la introducción que escribe para los viajes de Nicolás Tanco en 1861, la detestable moda del viaje a Europa que invade las sociedades hispanoamericanas.[39] La evocación de lo superficial del viaje placentero y

---

[38]   Adriano Páez publica en París la *Revista Latinoamericana* en 1874; Ricardo Pereira y Alberto Urdaneta la revista *Los Andes* en 1878-79.

[39]   'Si los facilidades para viajar seducen a los unos, las dificultades y la mayor distancia parece que empujan a los otros, sobre todo a los americanos del Sur, que invirtiendo la tendencia general de la emigración despueblan nuestra América para poblar la Europa; confundiendo así la oficina estadística que no puede explicarse el fenómeno del poco aumento de la población del nuevo mundo. Viejos, jóvenes, niños, mujeres, todos vienen a Europa, principalmente a París, en donde cada república ha

turístico, y de lo ridículo y pretencioso de los viajeros hispanoamericanos en
París, no es sino un tópico más de la literatura sobre Europa, que los mismos
viajeros difunden abundantemente.

Los términos del debate sobre el viaje a Europa, más allá de la crítica
sociológica, indican más bien en nuestro concepto que el discurso sobre Europa
se sitúa en el marco de otro debate, más esencial en la política interior: el de la
legitimidad nacional, por la que luchan y se oponen liberales y conservadores.
Revelan asímismo la existencia de una delicada articulacón entre un fenómeno
general de referencia a las naciones civilizadas del viejo mundo y las exigencias
de nacionalismo que impone la competencia por el poder político. El viaje a
Europa es 'legítimo' sólo en la medida en que se le otorga un valor pedagógico,
luego una utilidad patriótica. Los detractores del viaje dirigen siempre sus
ataques a la inutilidad de la experiencia europea en el contexto nacional de
Colombia; al cuestionar su utilidad, lo descalifican, lo hacen 'ilegítimo'.

Así, mientras que durante la segunda mitad del siglo XIX, el viaje a Europa
se institucionaliza en tanto característica social propia de las élites, sean
liberales o conservadoras, cada bando trata de desacreditar al otro en su
voluntad de acceder al poder a través del cuestionamiento de su patriotismo y del
cargo de europeismo, y luego de ilegitimidad nacional, que le lanza. Al mismo
tiempo que se afirma como signo distintivo de las élites, el discurso sobre
Europa cristaliza la polarizacion retórica que opone entre sí a las élites liberales
y a las élites conservadoras. De ahí nace este doble discurso sobre Europa que
se observa en el debate político colombiano: de un lado, un discurso pedagógico,
que es también un discurso de competencia, de poder, basado en la virtud
legitimadora de la experiencia europea, y que utiliza exageradamente el tema de
un patriotismo desinteresado y alejado de los conflictos partidarios, desarrollado
por la estadía en Europa (las luchas nacionales se presentan entonces como
propias a la infancia de la nación, mientras que la experiencia europea
corresponde a la madurez política); de otro lado, un discurso nacionalista de
rechazo a la influencia extranjera contra un adversario desacreditado por su
europeismo y su falta de legitimidad nacional.[40]

Los mismos hombres manejan este doble discurso. Discurso de competencia
y de poder, el discurso sobre Europa se transforma, cuando necesario, en
discurso de combate en la lucha por el poder. Discurso sobre la legitimidad

---

fundado una colonia en cuyo seno se cumplen todos los actos solemnes de la existencia: nacen,
crecen, se educan – así lo esperamos – se casan, se multiplican y hasta mueren.' Pedro María
Moure, introducción a Nicolás Tanco Armero, *Viaje a Nueva Granada a China y de China a Francia*
(París, 1861), pp. VI-VII.

[40]   En su estudio sobre la contienda electoral de 1875, Eduardo Posada-Carbó muestra cómo se acusa
al candidato Rafael Núñez, entonces recientemente regresado de su permanencia de 12 años en
Liverpool y El Havre, de no tener suficiente arraigo nacional. E. Posada-Carbó, 'Elections and civil
wars in nineteenth-century Colombia: the 1875 Presidential campaign', *Journal of Latin American
Studies*, Vol. 26, October 1994, pp. 621-49.

propia, se transforma en discurso sobre la ilegitimidad del otro. Esta paradoja aparente está sin duda estrechamente ligada a la doble exigencia que se impone a la clase política de una nación como Colombia en el siglo XIX: llevar al país a ocupar su rango en la asamblea de los países cultos, defender su integridad en tanto joven nación. Una doble exigencia que entraña una constante oscilación entre los dos polos de la representación de Europa: la experiencia europea que otorga la calificación, por lo tanto la capacidad necesaria para ejercer el poder político, y el 'europeismo' que tiende a quitar la legitimidad nacional, es decir, el derecho a ejercer el poder.

CHAPTER 4

Los partidos políticos en la argentina (1890-1914): programas y plataformas. El caso de la Liga del Sur

Carlos Malamud[*]

El objeto de este trabajo está vinculado a la figura de Lisandro de la Torre y a su trayectoria política. De la Torre, que actuó en la vida pública entre 1889 y 1939, impulsó la creación de la Liga del Sur (LS) en 1908. Se trataba de un partido de ámbito local, provincial, que funcionó en el Sur de la provincia de Santa Fe hasta 1916, cuando finalmente se disolvió para ingresar en el Partido Demócrata Progresista (PDP). En sus orígenes, el PDP (cuya fundación también fue impulsada por de la Torre), fue uno de los máximos esfuerzos de la época para crear un gran partido liberal-conservador de ámbito nacional.

Pese a todo lo que había en juego, la experiencia del PDP terminó fracasando debido a las posturas divergentes mantenidas por de la Torre y por el gobernador de la provincia de Buenos Aires, el conservador Marcelino Ugarte, a la existencia de concepciones políticas distintas y a los evidentes problemas de liderazgo. Sin embargo, esta interpretación resulta demasiado benévola con el resto de los protagonistas y debería ser matizada, ya que sólo carga las tintas sobre los dos personajes más notorios e intransigentes. Los problemas de liderazgo entre los restantes políticos con aspiraciones presidenciales involucrados en el proyecto (Julio A. Roca (h), Benito Villanueva y otros de igual nivel), la actitud mantenida por el presidente de la Plaza en sus esfuerzos por influir en el proceso político y en la designación de su sucesor y las cuestiones organizativas entre una serie de partidos provinciales que no habían perdido ni sus estructuras orgánicas ni sus señas de identidad fueron los principales obstáculos de un proyecto que de haberse consolidado podría haber cambiado el rumbo político del país.

En su momento, la LS fue presentada como el prototipo del 'partido programático', aunque también el Partido Socialista (PS) tuvo un programa estructurado. Uno de sus máximos dirigentes, Enrique Thedy, escribía en 1911, en la prestigiosa *Revista Argentina de Ciencia Política*, que:

'En la historia de los partidos políticos argentinos constituidos con posterioridad a la organización nacional, buscaríamos vanamente cuales han sido las ideas sociales, económicas, institucionales o de otro orden que los han separado en la lucha democrática. Sus programas apenas si

[*] Este trabajo fue escrito en el St. Antony's College (Oxford) gracias a una beca del Ministerio de Educación y Ciencia de España (Programa MEC-St. Antony's College). Agradezco los comentarios de Paula Alonso, Ezequiel Gallo y Eduardo Posada-Carbó.

divergen en la forma, el fondo de todos ellos es el mismo: la repetición de algunos principios axiomáticos de moral cívica, la promesa de impulsar el progreso del país, de garantizar la pureza del sufragio, etc.; en la vaga generalidad de sus términos, caben las soluciones más contradictorias y las tendencias más inconciliables. Para encontrar diferencia entre un partido y otros, tenemos que acudir a los nombres de sus miembros dirigentes, y nada más que a sus nombres, siendo frecuente una manifiesta anarquía de opiniones, entre los elementos de las juntas directivas, sobre cuestiones fundamentales de gobierno. Nuestros partidos políticos han sido, en su inmensa mayoría, netamente personalistas: la participación accidental que hayan podido tener en la resolución de ciertos problemas de carácter colectivo, no basta para cambiar su índole.'[1]

Las opiniones de Thedy constituyen una buena excusa inicial para hablar de los partidos políticos en la Argentina de fines del siglo XIX y principios del XX y especialmente de la LS. De ahí que estas páginas se centren, en primer lugar, en los partidos políticos actuantes en Argentina en esas fechas y luego en un breve análisis de la plataforma y características de la LS.

La regeneración de la política

En la segunda mitad del siglo XIX, la política, los políticos y los partidos políticos argentinos estaban bastante desprestigiados, aunque había algunas excepciones rescatables. Resulta bastante significativo el hecho de que el 9 de diciembre de 1861 el gobernador de la provincia de Salta, José María Todd, prohibiera por decreto la existencia de los partidos en su provincia, 'reputando sedicioso al que en adelante se declarara de algún bando', ya que 'los ciudadanos (debían ser) todos constitucionales, sumisos a la Constitución'.[2]

La actuación del Partido Autonomista Nacional (PAN), si bien permitió la consolidación política del país y su desarrollo económico, al mismo tiempo aumentó el malestar en algunos sectores de las élites nacionales y provinciales que no participaban directamente de la gestión pública. Sin embargo, el desembarco del juarismo en la arena nacional terminó liquidando una vieja manera de hacer política e impuso un nuevo estilo, mucho más audaz, que dejó

---

[1] Enrique Thedy, 'Indole y propósitos de la Liga del Sur', *Revista Argentina de Ciencia Política* (RACP), Vol. 1 (1911), p. 76. El artículo de Thedy está casi íntegramente basado en la 'Petición de Reformas Constitucionales y Legislativas', presentada por la LS en mayo de 1909 a la Legislatura de Santa Fe. Con ocasión de las elecciones del 31 de marzo (gobernador y vice de la provincia) y del 7 de abril de 1912 (diputados nacionales), el diario rosarino *La Capital* (LC) publicó a principio de marzo una serie de notas, bajo el título global de 'Asuntos del día', donde explicaba y comentaba la plataforma electoral de la LS, que extractan los dos materiales más arriba mencionados.

[2] Carlos Melo, *Los partidos políticos argentinos* (Córdoba, 1945, 1ª ed., 1943), p. 15.

en la cuneta a un gran número de descontentos.[3] La visión negativa de la vida política argentina responde en buena medida a los testimonios de aquellas personas que quedaron marginadas o postergadas en este proceso.

Paralela a esa visión tan negativa de la gestión de la cosa pública surgió una especie de regeneracionismo dispuesto a erradicar los vicios imperantes en el sistema político, con una retórica que luego haría suyo el radicalismo. La 'Juventud' encarnaba uno de los símbolos regeneracionistas. De ahí que cuando en 1889 se creó ese gran conglomerado opositor del que posteriormente surgiría la Unión Cívica Radical (UCR), su primera denominación fue la de Unión Cívica de la Juventud. Años más tarde, en torno a 1899/1900, Lisandro de la Torre fundó en Rosario el Partido de la Juventud, con el fin de oponerse a lo que él entendía como política fraudulenta del gobernador Iturraspe.[4]

En el discurso fundacional de la LS, de la Torre señaló que 'La Liga del Sur se organiza, sin banderas partidarias, como una reunión y reacción de las malas leyes que causan los malos gobiernos'.[5] Como se ve, en la primera década del siglo XX, la visión negativa, casi peyorativa, de la política seguía pesando en aquellos que aparecían con planteos regeneracionistas. El regeneracionismo de la Liga se expresaba de forma permanente en afirmaciones como las siguientes: la Liga no busca 'situaciones de mando, sino la regeneración de nuestras costumbres políticas';[6] 'la base de nuestra política es completamente nueva y muy al revés de esa rutinaria política caudillesca' o 'a las urnas iremos como hemos ido y como van los pueblos que tienen cultura, porque nuestras únicas armas son: el programa y el voto. No conspiramos contra nadie, ni prometemos vengarnos de nadie cuando lleguemos al poder'.[7] En las elecciones a gobernador del 31 de marzo de 1912 la Liga llamó al voto, pero en un manifiesto se limitó a fundamentar la necesidad del sufragio, 'cualquiera que sea la lista a que se inclinen las preferencias individuales'.[8] En cierto sentido, el 'regeneracionismo' de de la Torre es heredero del radicalismo alemanista, al que estuvo vinculado hasta su ruptura con la UCR en 1897.

De acuerdo con algunas definiciones al uso, como la de William Chamber, seguida también por Karen Remmer, la existencia de una plataforma política es

---

[3]   Ver William T. Duncan, 'Government by Audacity. Politics and the Argentine Economy, 1885-1892', PhD Thesis, University of Melbourne, 1981.

[4]   Plácido Grela, *Alcorta. Origen y desarrollo del pueblo y de la rebelión agraria de 1912* (Rosario, 1975), pp. 79-84.

[5]   Discurso de Lisandro de la Torre (en adelante LDLT) del 29 noviembre 1908, en Rosario; *La Capital*, 30 noviembre 1908.

[6]   *La Capital*, 1 abril 1912.

[7]   'Manifiesto del Comité "10 de febrero" de la LS a la juventud estudiosa de Rosario', en *La Capital*, 31 marzo 1912.

[8]   *La Capital*, 30 marzo 1912.

un elemento decisivo para poder definir un partido político y esto, junto a otras características, como las relaciones mediatizadas entre los líderes y la militancia a través de estructuras partidarias, es lo que permite diferenciarlos de otros grupos políticos.[9] Surge aquí un problema serio en torno a la definición de los partidos que actúan dentro de sistemas que podríamos caracterizar como oligárquicos o caciquiles pero que participan con cierta frecuencia en las convocatorias electorales.

Hasta 1890, los diferentes partidos o grupos políticos (dejemos abierto el interrogante) que actuaban en la vida política argentina se caracterizaron por el caudillismo y el personalismo; por la puesta en marcha de las estructuras partidarias y electorales coincidiendo con las convocatorias a las urnas; por la inexistencia de programas políticos coherentes y cuanto mucho por la promulgación de una plataforma de gobierno, una especie de programa, que recogía las principales acciones que se desarrollarían desde el poder; por la inexistencia de organismos de gobierno del partido (comités, centrales, secretarías, etc.), ya que su lugar era ocupado por los caudillos locales y provinciales y por la inexistencia de un sistema de convenciones que permitiera a los afiliados elegir democráticamente a los candidatos que los iban a representar. En su lugar, éstos eran designados por el presidente, el gobernador saliente o por las autoridades directamente implicadas en la contienda.

Desde la perspectiva que a nosotros nos interesa habría que diferenciar en primer lugar lo que es un partido con programa de un simple programa de gobierno, que era lo que solían presentar la mayor parte de los candidatos a elecciones presidenciales o de gobernador. Pero hasta esa plataforma electoral o de gobierno era redactada por el candidato ya que no solía haber instancias permanentes adecuadas para que los afiliados discutieran esas cuestiones. A veces ni siquiera así ocurrían las cosas. En noviembre de 1897, el santafesino José Bernardo Iturraspe se quejaba de que no había tenido tiempo suficiente para desarrollar un programa de gobierno para su próxima gobernación.[10]

En la Argentina previa a 1890 el panorama se complica por la práctica inexistencia de partidos nacionales. El PAN ocupaba el centro de la escena y la mayor parte de los conflictos ocurrían en su interior, entre los distintos grupos que competían por el poder, y no fuera de él. Quizá se podría hablar del PAN como del primer gran movimiento político argentino que desde su creación en 1870 englobaba casi toda la vida política del país. Rivarola había definido al PAN como una 'vasta asociación sin contrato ni reglamento, sin estatutos y sin programa de todos los gobernantes, legisladores, jueces y demás funcionarios

---

[9]   Karen Remmer, *Party Competition in Argentina and Chile. Political Recruitment and Public Policy, 1890-1930* (Lincoln, Neb., 1984), p. 8.

[10]   Arthur F. Liebscher, 'Commercial Expansion and Political Change: Santa Fe Province, 1897-1916', tesis doctoral inédita, Indiana University, 1975, p. 59.

nacionales y provinciales'.[11] Según Botana, se trataba de una organización nacional que representaba una madeja de vínculos entre notables de origen local y que tenía muchas semejanzas con el partido federalista de Hamilton, de fines del siglo XVIII.[12] Para Peck, el PAN era una coalición no demasiado férrea en lo que se refiere a sus miembros y de una naturaleza híbrida que reflejaba con precisión el equilibrio entre la política nacional y provincial y cuya principal función era establecer un marco adecuado para la solución de las disputas provinciales. Si pudo sobrevivir tantos años se debió a que su existencia suponía muy poco más que la supervivencia de un reducido grupo de líderes nacionales y a su éxito en reducir la separación existente entre los partidos de la capital y los del interior.[13]

Cabe preguntarse, sin embargo, si la conformación tan deforme observada en el plano nacional también se reproducía en las provincias o si, por el contrario, en algunas de ellas se pueden encontrar estructuras partidarias más cohesionadas, estructuras orgánicas más desarrolladas. Sólo nuevos estudios de ámbito regional podrán aclarar este interrogante. Vale la pena recordar, de todas formas, la perfecta simbiosis existente entre el gobierno nacional y los gobiernos provinciales. Unos y otros se necesitaban mutuamente y esa necesidad reforzaba una alianza de hierro. Esto no implica que no hubiera lealtades cruzadas (gobernadores partidarios de Juárez Celman en momentos en que Roca pretendía recuperar el control del PAN después de la revolución de 1890) o numerosas fricciones, muchas veces saldadas con la intervención federal a las provincias más díscolas.

Si en el PAN se observan estas características, ¿qué puede decirse entonces de otros partidos, mucho más transitorios o coyunturales, generalmente apoyados en la figura de algún personaje que se sentía excluido del PAN? Este puede ser el caso de los diferentes partidos republicanos (Del Valle, Emilio Mitre) o liberales (Bartolomé Mitre, Tejedor, Ocampo). La mayor parte de las veces, estos partidos no sobrevivían a las derrotas electorales. Un ejemplo es el de los Partidos Unidos, una coalición electoral de diferentes facciones y personalidades porteñas opuestas a Juárez Celman: la Unión Católica, que había lanzado en 1885 la candidatura de Manuel Gorostiaga; Aristóbulo del Valle, que propuso a Dardo Rocha; Bernardo de Irigoyen y sus seguidores y Mitre y su Partido Liberal. Dentro de la coalición reinaba una mutua desconfianza, a tal punto que los mitristas vetaron la candidatura de Irigoyen y éste hizo lo propio con la de Mitre. Cada grupo mantuvo su organización partidaria de forma independiente. El candidato de consenso, una figura anodina, fue Manuel Ocampo

---

[11] Rodolfo Rivarola, 'Crónica', *Revista Argentina de Ciencia Política*, Año I, No. 5, p. 682, cit. por Natalio Botana, *El orden conservador. La política argentina entre 1880 y 1916* (Buenos Aires, 1977), p. 224.

[12] Botana, *El orden conservador*, p. 245.

[13] Donald Peck: 'Argentinian Politics and the Province of Mendoza, 1890-1916', PhD Thesis, Universidad de Oxford, 1977, p. 15.

y sólo Salta, Buenos Aires y Tucumán votaron contra Juárez. Después de la derrota, la coalición se disolvió.[14]

En la década de 1890 se crearon dos partidos de alcance nacional, la UCR y el Partido Socialista, PS, con repercusiones duraderas en la historia política argentina, aunque de carácter bastante diferente. La Unión Cívica de la Juventud dio lugar a la Unión Cívica (UC), después de la Asamblea Popular del 13 de abril de 1890 en el Frontón de Buenos Aires. En este movimiento, que concluiría con la creación de la UC Nacional y de la UCR, se fue produciendo una clarificación política en el conglomerado porteño de descontentos anti-PAN que fundaron la UC, un conglomerado sumamente heterogéneo que iba desde católicos hasta liberales.

En noviembre de 1892 se dictó la 'Carta Orgánica Nacional' de la UCR, en cuyo preámbulo se señalaba que se trataba de una asociación política impersonal formada para luchar 'por el resurgimiento de la vida institucional, que asegure a la patria su paz y su progreso, por el cumplimiento honrado de la ley, la pureza de la moral administrativa, el ejercicio efectivo de la soberanía popular, y el amplio reconocimiento de la autonomía de los Estados y de los municipios'.[15] El partido debía gobernarse por una Convención Nacional, que debía elegir a los candidatos a presidente y vicepresidente. Esa misma convención debía sancionar el Programa partidario veinticuatro horas antes de la denominación de los candidatos mencionados.

Las intentonas revolucionarias de 1890 y 1893 influyeron decisivamente sobre el perfil de la UCR y la muerte de Alem aceleró la crisis en el interior del partido, vinculada con el tipo de participación política que debía mantenerse.[16] La intransigencia, liderada por Hipólito Yrigoyen y que contó con la oposición de de la Torre, proclamaría en 1897 que la revolución era 'el único medio para conquistar la libertad del sufragio'.[17]

Ezequiel Gallo y Silvia Sigal han afirmado que el programa radical se agotaba 'consciente y deliberadamente, en la lucha por la participación política'. Hipólito Yrigoyen escribía en 1909: 'extraviados viven los que piden programas a la Causa Reivindicadora', y que la falta de programa no es un defecto sino una virtud del Partido Radical. Por ello, el día que se lograse el funcionamiento de las instituciones, el Partido Radical 'concretará más su programa inicial con fórmulas que, traducidas en funciones de gobierno de legalidad que entonces han

---

[14] Paula Alonso, 'The Origins of the Argentine Radical Party, 1889-1898', tesis doctoral inédita, Universidad de Oxford, 1992, pp. 62-4.

[15] Melo, *Los partidos políticos*, p. 31.

[16] Alonso, 'The Origins of the Argentine Radical Party', p. 302.

[17] Melo, *Los partidos políticos*, p. 32.

de existir, pueden ser benéficas'.[18] Con Yrigoyen, el programa radical, la causa, era la revolución y la abstención electoral.

Al finalizar 1904, en una reunión con correligionarios santafesinos, Yrigoyen señaló que la acción revolucionaria no debía ser interferida por la crítica de los 'partidos militantes', que los acusaban de carecer de un programa concreto. La reparación nacional no puede encerrarse en los límites de un programa, ya que los abarca y sobrepasa. Los programas, señalaba Yrigoyen, vendrán después que el país incorpore el voto garantido y libre y:

'Aunque el triunfo parcial se les ofrezca por esos conglomerados esporádicos que se organizan para conquistar el poder y lo crean ustedes seguro, no vacilen en despreciarlo'.[19]

En 1894 se creó el PS, muy influido por organizaciones europeas similares y por los inmigrantes afiliados a las mismas que habían llegado a la Argentina en los años anteriores. En abril de 1895 se sancionó la Carta Orgánica del PS, que planteaba favorecer, con todos los medios a su alcance, la organización gremial de la clase trabajadora y la unión de los socialistas del mundo. Siendo fieles a su tradición, los socialistas argentinos se dieron rápidamente un programa mínimo, que en lo político propiciaba el sufragio universal sin distinción de sexos, el sistema electoral proporcional con representación de las minorías, la autonomía municipal, la justicia gratuita y jurados electivos, la separación de la Iglesia del Estado, la abolición de la deuda pública y la supresión del ejército permanente. Dentro de las medidas sociales y económicas, abogaban por la reglamentación de la jornada de trabajo, el salario mínimo, el descanso semanal obligatorio, la instrucción laica, gratuita y obligatoria, la abolición de los impuestos indirectos y la supresión de la herencia.[20]

La Liga del Sur: perfil social y político

Al margen del PS, por consiguiente, ningún otro partido salvo la LS, poseía un ideario político tan claramente definido y expresado en un programa partidario y una plataforma electoral. Es importante recalcar que el programa de la LS, aprobado por el órgano partidario establecido a tal efecto, fue levantado en todas las elecciones a las que concurría la Liga y que era defendido por sus representantes electos en los foros correspondientes (concejos deliberantes, legislatura

[18] Ezequiel Gallo y Silvia Sigal, 'La formación de los partidos políticos contemporáneos: la UCR (1890-1916)', en Torcuato Di Tella, Gino Germani, Jorge Graciarena et al, *Argentina, sociedad de masas* (Buenos Aires, 1966), pp. 130-1.

[19] Ricardo Caballero, *Hipólito Yrigoyen y la revolución radical de 1905* (Buenos Aires, 1975), p. 51.

[20] Melo, *Los partidos políticos*, p. 37.

provincial, Congreso nacional). La falta de partidos programáticos aparece mucho más clara en aquellos grupos ubicados en el centro político y la derecha, incluido el radicalismo. El diario *La Capital*, de Rosario, que apoyaba totalmente a la LS, señalaba en marzo de 1912 que:

'Como partido orgánico y de principios permanentes, no hay un solo problema provincial importante que no haya preocupado hondamente a la Liga del Sur; y por cierto que ninguno de ellos ha dejado de ser satisfactoriamente dilucidado a la luz del más patriótico de los análisis y de la más científica de las orientaciones. Se diferencia, pues, no sólo por sustentar principios concretos de gobierno y de ética política, sino también por la trascendental y benéfica pujanza de su acción, jamás inerte o desviada; y como la casta de políticos profesionales que ve en el puesto público la holganza y el acomodo personal bien remunerado es repudiada por su índole y propósitos, hasta en eso se distingue de sus adversarios, al entender que la política debe ser la dedicación de todos y el oficio de ninguno; bien es verdad que todo es cuestión de educación y de hábitos. La Liga del Sur pretende la representación de todas las opiniones en el gobierno de la provincia y que el manejo de la cosa pública tenga su origen en el pueblo; que éste ejerza la presión de su fuerza, conscientemente orientada en el sentido de que sus derechos, sus intereses y su vida se hallen a cubierto de las asechanzas que los políticos profesionales le tiendan en sus ansias de predominio tradicional.'[21]

Pese a contar con un programa coherente y un conjunto de estructuras y autoridades establecidas, la figura de Lisandro de la Torre imponía claramente su impronta sobre el conjunto del partido. Desde mucho tiempo antes de la fundación de la Liga, de la Torre estuvo forjando su liderazgo en Rosario, un liderazgo que sería indiscutible. Por su agresividad y su barba muy rubia en su ciudad natal lo llamaban 'el gato amarillo'.[22] A partir de 1912, y desde su puesto de diputado nacional, trató de difundir la plataforma de su partido impulsando algunos proyectos de ley (división y colonización de tierras, naturalización de extranjeros) de consumo directo por aquellos grupos sociales que eran el principal respaldo de su partido. Junto a de la Torre había otros líderes carismáticos como Enrique Thedy o Francisco Correa. En 1906 de la Torre era presidente de la Comisión rosarina de Defensa Agrícola y el 6 de junio de 1908 fue elegido presidente de la Sociedad Rural de Rosario.[23]

---

[21] *La Capital*, 30 marzo 1912.

[22] Raúl Larra, *Lisandro de la Torre. Vida y drama del solitario de Piñas* (Buenos Aires, 1942), p. 113.

[23] Archivo de la Sociedad Rural de Rosario, 'Libro de Actas de la Sociedad Rural de Rosario', Acta No. 418 del 6 junio 1908, p. 328.

Además de estos antecedentes, la Liga Liberal, creada para oponerse a la creación del obispado en Rosario, a principios de 1908, sirvió también de preámbulo a la Liga del Sur. Fue presidida inicialmente por Perfecto Araya, que había participado con de la Torre en la Unión Provincial de Santa Fe y el vicepresidente fue Carlos Paganini, pariente de de la Torre. También figuraban algunos dirigentes que tendrían una destacada actuación en la LS, como Enzo Bordabehere. A la asamblea fundacional acudieron los presidentes de las logias masónicas, sociedades gremiales y centros de estudiantes.[24]

En el momento de su fundación, la LS se benefició del vacío dejado en el espectro 'centrista' por el rotundo fracaso de la intentona revolucionaria de la UCR de 1905, que obligó a volver a las catacumbas a la organización provincial del radicalismo. Otros grupos de la oposición, como el liderado por de la Torre, ocuparon así ese vacío político. En noviembre de 1908 se comenzó a trabajar en la formación de un partido, para lo cual se creó una comisión integrada, entre otros, por Joaquín Legarza, Pedro Sánchez, José Castagnino y Lisandro de la Torre. El intento contó con la oposición de los diarios oficialistas de la capital provincial que atacaron a 'los comerciantes y demás caballeros rosarinos que han adherido con plausible entusiasmo al nuevo partido en formación'.[25] Pese a ello, el 20 de noviembre de 1908 se fundó la Liga del Sur.[26] El 29 de noviembre, en el teatro Opera, se celebró el primer acto público de la nueva agrupación donde, junto a otros, intervino de la Torre.[27]

Desde un primer momento la Liga se mostró contraria al recurso revolucionario y optó en su lugar por la movilización popular (actos públicos, manifestaciones): 'Donde no hay sufragio, la prensa y el meeting son los más eficaces medios de expresión de la voluntad popular.'[28] Decía de la Torre en el discurso pronunciado con ocasión de la creación de la Liga:

'He ahí nuestra misión: hacer de esa fuerza que nace el torrente de maña-na... En vez de repeler la fuerza con la fuerza acudamos con la razón. Hagamos el torrente por el convencimiento y la propaganda. Desde la Constitución inglesa hasta la emancipación americana las grandes reformas institucionales se han obtenido por la resistencia de los pueblos a soportar exacciones injustas.'[29]

---

[24]   *El Municipio* (EM) (Rosario), 8 y 11 agosto 1908.

[25]   *La Capital*, 17 noviembre 1908.

[26]   R. Caballero, en *Hipólito Yrigoyen*, p. 51, señala que en 1904 ya existía la Liga del Sur, probablemente confundido por la presentación como candidato independiente de Lisandro de la Torre a las elecciones de diputados nacionales de ese año.

[27]   *La Capital*, 26 noviembre 1908.

[28]   *La Capital*, 22 julio 1910.

[29]   Discurso de LDLT del 29 noviembre 1908, Rosario; *La Capital* (Rosario), 30 noviembre 1908.

En abril de 1910 la Liga insistió en algunas de sus reformas institucionales y para ello se propuso iniciar un período de 'saludable agitación', con reuniones y 'una gran manifestación callejera',[30] que se celebraría el 24 de julio,[31] lo que habla de la gran preparación de la campaña y la planificación de las actividades políticas. Las reformas consistían en: cambios de la Constitución provincial; autonomía municipal; elección de intendentes; elección de senadores en función de la población; voto para los extranjeros; consejos escolares electivos y autónomos; representación de la minoría; nuevo censo provincial; anexión a la circunscripción judicial del Sur de los departamentos de San Martín y San Jerónimo; igualdad en la representación y en las cargas (la LS no es regionalista); comicios libres; mejora del nivel educativo de la Provincia.[32] Para impulsar estas reformas de la Torre se entrevistó con el ministro de Gobierno de la provincia, Estanislao López.[33] Se nota aquí una cierta habilidad a la hora de compatibilizar la presión en la calle con la negociación y también la preocupación por salir en la prensa.

Ante la presión continua de la Liga, el gobierno provincial señaló que propiciaba muchas de las reivindicaciones de la Liga, como la autonomía municipal y su participación en la gestión de los ingresos fiscales obtenidos de las patentes y contribuciones directas; el nombramiento de los jueces de paz por ternas y la designación del número de parlamentarios de forma proporcional a la población. También se plantearon dificultades para que los intendentes fueran elegidos por el Consejo Deliberante de cada municipalidad en vez de ser designados por el gobernador, ya que ello requería la reforma de la Constitución provincial.[34] El acercamiento del gobierno a las posturas de la Liga fue mal visto por algunos sectores de Santa Fe, como el periódico *La Opinión*.[35]

En cierta medida, el fenómeno de la LS no debe verse como un hecho aislado en la política argentina en torno al 'Centenario'. En varias provincias comenzaron a surgir partidos locales que trataban de aprovechar el espacio que se abría para la oposición, debido fundamentalmente al inexorable resquebrajamiento de esa gran máquina política que había sido el PAN. En el caso de la LS, y en menor medida en algunos partidos departamentales de Córdoba, estos grupos se centraban en la política municipal y en los asuntos locales, en particular la incidencia de los impuestos. Según Peck, fue en las provincias pampeanas donde esta forma de hacer política encontró su expresión más clara y en la provincia de Buenos Aires donde la política municipal llegó

---

[30] *La Capital*, 1 abril 1910.

[31] *La Capital*, 21 julio 1910.

[32] *La Capital*, 22 julio 1910.

[33] *La Capital*, 17 abril 1910.

[34] *La Capital*, 14 mayo 1910.

[35] *La Capital*, 18 mayo 1910.

inclusive a adoptar la forma de protestas violentas. Este tipo de partidos también se desarrolló en algunas provincias pequeñas, como Mendoza, aunque con señas de identidad más desdibujadas.[36]

La LS reclamaba el desarrollo de la zona Sur de la provincia de Santa Fe, postergada por el Norte, debido al protagonismo de la capital provincial, Santa Fe. El nuevo partido se nutrió fundamentalmente de la ciudad de Rosario, cuyo acelerado crecimiento había favorecido la competencia con la capital. Sin embargo, de la Torre no presentó a su partido como dispuesto al enfrentamiento:

'La Liga del Sur no es la liga del sur contra la del norte. La Liga del Sur es la concentración de voluntades de los habitantes del sur en defensa de su autonomía y en contra del localismo absorbente de la ciudad capital.'[37] 'Mañana podría existir la Liga del Norte con la misma bandera, porque también el norte ignora lo que es gobierno propio, representación política y libertad electoral.'[38]

El radicalismo acusaba de regionalismo a la Liga. En respuesta a tal acusación, en un discurso durante la campaña para la elección de gobernador en Santa Fé en 1912, de la Torre se preguntaba:

'¿Quiénes son los regionalistas: ellos, los radicales, o nosotros? ¿Nosotros porque queremos en el gobierno a los hombres del Sur o ellos que no los admiten?'[39]

La Liga reclamaba la capitalidad de la provincia para Rosario, señalando que 'representamos el espíritu nacional contra el espíritu local, el espíritu argentino contra el espíritu santafesino de la ciudad capital. Y porque no tememos al extranjero lo llamamos a colaborar, seguros de asimilarlo'.[40] El programa de la Liga desarrolla en buena medida las concepciones federalistas y comunalistas de de la Torre, que habían sido previamente expuestas en su tesis doctoral.[41]

Para Natalio Botana, la Liga del Sur puede ser vista como un movimiento de protesta del Sur de Santa Fe contra el predominio del Norte y de la capital. El Sur de la provincia, que concentraba el 62% del capital provincial, estaba en el apogeo de su expansión gracias al arrendamiento de tierras y tenía un crecido

---

[36] D. Peck, 'Argentinian Politics and the Province of Mendoza, 1890-1916', p. 135.

[37] Discurso de LDLT del 29 noviembre 1908; *La Capital*, 30 noviembre 1908.

[38] *La Capital*, 16 febrero 1912.

[39] *La Capital*, 16 febrero 1912.

[40] R. Larra, *Lisandro de la Torre. Vida y drama del solitario de Pinas* (Buenos Aires, 1942), p. 110.

[41] Larra, *Lisandro de la Torre*, p. 112.

número de inmigrantes extranjeros (39,7%). El aparato político de la Liga tenía un fuerte apoyo electoral en el Sur de la provincia, donde en 1912 obtuvo el 42,4% de los votos.[42] La liga también puede verse como un partido que proponía nuevas reformas en el sistema institucional santafesino, las que podían extenderse al resto del país.

En los hechos, el principal enemigo de de la Torre y de la LS fue la UCR más que el norte de la Provincia. En parte, por la ruptura de de la Torre con el radicalismo, pero también porque competían por el mismo electorado. Inicialmente la LS se había nutrido de algunos radicales, ante la abstención de la UCR a participar en las luchas electorales.[43]

Por aquel entonces de la Torre estaba subyugado por la experiencia del gobierno local en los Estados Unidos. Sus referencias a la situación de Estados Unidos o a políticos norteamericanos, como Wilson, son abundantes.[44] De la Torre era además lector de Tocqueville y admirador de Sarmiento. Como él mismo lo expresó en el discurso de presentación de su partido: 'Tomad una Constitución cualquiera de un Estado Americano: policía, justicia de paz, instrucción primaria, caminos, etc., todo eso es resorte local', mientras que en Argentina tanto la administración como la política provincial se hallan bajo 'la centralización del Poder Ejecutivo y la sumisa burocracia'.[45]

De la Torre pensaba que había que buscar la raíz de los males argentinos en la centralización creciente de los gobiernos provinciales, lo que engendraba oligarquía. La Liga era un 'partido de ideas y de libre discusión', pero teniendo en cuenta que su fuerte impronta ideológica no desdeñaba los intereses económicos como substrato de apoyo político.[46] En su primer discurso en el Congreso de la Nación, de la Torre comparó la legislación argentina con la de los Estados Unidos, insistiendo en los temas de la educación primaria, la justicia, y el gobierno local.[47]

En la reunión inaugural de la Liga se dio a conocer una plataforma de ocho puntos, que constituye el primer programa de la agrupación:

1º La reforma amplia de la constitución provincial.

---

[42] Botana, *El orden conservador*, p. 316.

[43] *El Municipio*, 25 abril 1911.

[44] Ver *La Capital*, 20 enero 1913.

[45] Discurso de LDLT del 29 noviembre 1908, Rosario; *La Capital*, 30 noviembre 1908.

[46] Botana, *El orden conservador*, p. 316.

[47] Discurso en la Cámara de Diputados, 1 junio 1912.

2º La reforma de la composición del Colegio Electoral y del Senado Provincial, haciéndolos electivos en proporción a la población, y la ejecución del segundo censo de la Provincia.

3º La concesión a cada distrito rural del derecho de elegir por el voto de los vecinos contribuyentes, nacionales y extranjeros, las autoridades policiales, la comisión de fomento, la justicia de paz y un Consejo Escolar.

4º La autonomía municipal para las ciudades del Rosario y Casilda; intendente municipal electivo, nueva ley electoral que establezca la representación de las minorías y limite el derecho electoral activo a los que paguen una cuota determinada de impuesto.

5º Reconocimiento a cada localidad de un tanto por ciento de la contribución directa que se recaude en ella en beneficio de sus rentas locales.

6º Anexión de los departamentos San Martín y San Jerónimo a la circunscripción electoral del Sur.

7º Reforma del sistema tributario sobre la base de hacer libre el trabajo.

8º Inamovilidad de los jueces.[48]

Para José Ingenieros, la Liga representaba los intereses de la burguesía argentina en lucha contra los privilegios feudales.[49] Para Larra, el biógrafo de de la Torre próximo al Partido Comunista, la LS era visto como un movimiento propiciado por las 'fuerzas vivas' de Rosario, que estaban oprimidas por la burocracia del Norte de la provincia: cerealistas, industriales, comerciantes y colonos ricos, la 'expresión típica de la burguesía capitalista'. Así se ve a la Liga como un partido de 'gente de orden'. Para reforzar esta idea se menciona la organización de una manifestación de cuadra y media de extensión, encabezada por de la Torre, con 'personas cubiertas de galeras de felpa', lo que resulta 'harto sospechoso para el criollaje de extramuros y de desheredados de todas las zonas que permanecen al margen de la agrupación', de modo tal que 'la liturgia de las galeras de pelo ha de pesar como un lastre en la futura carrera política' de de la Torre. Larra ubica la sede de la Liga del Sur en el aristocrático Club Social de Rosario,[50] aunque en realidad la secretaría del Comité Rosario estaba en San Luis 1440.[51] La manifestación se celebró el 3 de enero de 1909 y figura como uno de los hitos fundacionales de la Liga, que en ese momento se veía obligada a dar respuestas efectistas. Para La Capital, 'todo el Rosario en sus elementos más significativos estuvo presente'.[52]

---

[48] Larra, Lisandro de la Torre, pp. 109-10.

[49] José Ingenieros, Sociología argentina, cit. por R. Larra, Lisandro de la Torre, p. 112.

[50] Larra, Lisandro de la Torre, p. 111.

[51] La Capital, 6 septiembre 1913.

[52] La Capital, 29 noviembre 1912.

Ha habido algunos intentos de comparar a de la Torre con José Batlle y Ordóñez. Hay que tener en cuenta, sin embargo, algunas diferencias fundamentales. En primer lugar, Batlle apostó por la renovación de uno de los partidos tradicionales, el Colorado, y no por el principismo regeneracionista del Partido Constitucional. En segundo lugar, está el episodio de las 'galeras', resuelto de manera distinta por cada uno de los dos personajes. Decía Batlle, en abril de 1887, a propósito de una manifestación que se organizaba en Montevideo:

'Han dicho algunos, haciendo por ello un cargo al Partido Colorado, que en la manifestación se veían pocas levitas y pocas galeras. Es cierto: en el Partido Colorado, predomina el elemento del pueblo, las clases trabajadoras.'

Para Grompone, está ahí la síntesis de su programa futuro: el abandono de la clase intelectual o acomodada, de los hombres de 'levita y galera' para tener a su lado a los desheredados y a los que tienen necesidad de protección. Hay en todo ello una nueva convicción democrática y una obra de táctica.'[53]

Una vez fundada, la Liga pretendió consolidar su presencia en el Sur de la provincia y en este sentido repitió el esquema radical fundando comités en los distintos pueblos.[54] Desde un principio, la Liga debió luchar contra la oposición de las autoridades provinciales y locales.[55] Los candidatos electorales de la Liga, cualquiera fuera su importancia, eran designados por una Convención electoral.

Un tema central de la LS y de su programa político, que ha merecido numerosas interpretaciones sobre la composición de la Liga y los sectores sociales que la respaldaban, es su reivindicación de los derechos políticos de los extranjeros (en la Liga militaban muchos hijos de inmigrantes). Hay que tener en cuenta que en términos relativos, Santa Fe fue la provincia que absorbió el

---

[53] Antonio Grompone, *La ideología de Batlle* (Montevideo, 1967), pp. 40-1 y 43. Dice el mismo Grompone: 'Para el Partido Constitucional no podía existir la justificación racional de los partidos tradicionales y por eso debían ser desechados para ir a la defensa de los principios constitucionales puros y de la descentralización administrativa como fórmula que diera directamente a los pueblos influencia en el gobierno. La concepción de Batlle difiere de ésta porque no parte de la transfiguración radical por obra de las doctrinas y porque se coloca en la otra posición que tendía previamente a crear las fuerzas que debían hacer posibles las reformas de los gobiernos. Estas fuerzas están en los partidos políticos que deben tener necesariamente una corriente de sentimientos y de tradición que no puede ni debe despreciarse. Estas fuerzas no se organizan con un designio preconcebido sino que van surgiendo por la obra continuada de la propaganda racional y de la acción misma. El tribuno no debe ser el hombre de la palabra arrebatadora, sino el hombre que convence', pp. 44-5.

[54] El 7 febrero 1908 se instalaron comités en los pueblos de Bustinza y Correa. A ambos actos asistió LDLT; *La Capital*, 6 febrero 1909.

[55] *La Capital*, 7 febrero 1909.

mayor número de inmigrantes,[56] y si de la Torre quería hacer una política nueva, con un partido moderno, debía forzosamente contar con los inmigrantes:

'En la Liga del Sur no solo se encuentra inscripto el ciudadano que tiene voto para elegir diputados y senadores, sino también el que elige representantes a la Comuna; esto quiere decir que no es sólo el nacido en esta tierra el que se encuentra afiliado a la Liga del Sur, sino también el extranjero, el extranjero que trabaja, el extranjero que produce.'[57]

Este hecho le valió a la Liga el apodo de 'extranjerizante' o 'partido de los gringos', denominación que luego heredaría el PDP.[58] A principios de agosto de 1913 de la Torre presentó al parlamento un proyecto de ley sobre naturalización de extranjeros.

Sin embargo, la Liga también sacaba a relucir sus raíces criollas. Así es como *La Capital* publicó la siguiente creación del payador Máximo Castro, del pueblo de Serodino, que también incluye en su canto una alusión a los extranjeros:

'Que vaya en alas del viento
(Diligente mensajero)
Este cantar con que quiero
Expresarles lo que siento
Ya que ha llegado el momento
De desembuchar el rollo;
Que como liguista y criollo
Yo ni me engaño ni miento.

Con el corazón henchido
De patriótico entusiasmo
Para acompañar mi canto
Voy la guitarra a pulsar;
Y en un puñado de flores,
Con estos versos sinceros,
Argentinos y extranjeros
Quiero orgulloso enlazar.

Pues todos son en la patria
Un mismo brazo fornido

---

[56] Ver, Ezequiel Gallo, 'Conflictos socio-políticos en las colonias agrícolas de Santa Fe (1870-1880)', Documento de Trabajo, Instituto Torcuato Di Tella, Centro de Investigaciones Sociales, No. 87, Buenos Aires, 1973.

[57] 'Manifiesto del Comité "10 de febrero" de la LS a la juventud estudiosa de Rosario', en *La Capital*, 31 marzo 1912.

[58] Larra, *Lisandro de la Torre*, p. 111.

Que trabaja decidido
Bajo el paño bicolor.
Y han nombrado a de la Torre
Ese caudillo arrogante,
Egregio representante
De su unánime opinión.

A todos los partidarios
Hoy les quiero recordar,
Que el 31 de marzo
Tendremos que sufragar
Y si queremos, hermanos,
El triunfo de la virtud,
Votemos por de la Torre
Y por la Liga del Sur.

Frente a frente nos veremos
Con los antiguos mandones
Que no tienen ni nociones,
¡Verán como son más fuertes
Que las hordas oligárquicas
Nuestras huestes democráticas
Que anhelan la libertad!

Y aquí les pido disculpa
Por no continuar payando,
Pues termino saludando
Al color blanco y azul;
Y también a mis amigos
Y a todos mis superiores,
Y por último señores,
¡Viva la Liga del Sur![59]

A pesar de estas innegables expresiones criollas, la Liga fue acusada de utilizar el tema de los extranjeros con propósitos electorales. Los radicales reprocharon a la Liga que cuando se supo que las elecciones a diputados nacionales de 1912 serían con el padrón de 1911, ésta

'tomó sobre sí la ingrata tarea de nacionalizar extranjeros de cualquier origen y condición, con fines electorales. Dicho partido organizó oficinas independientes de sus locales, tanto en Rosario como en algunos departamentos del sur, encargados del reclutamiento de extranjeros. Se dio el caso visible de un grupo de hindúes que accidentalmente había quedado

---

[59] *La Capital*, 29 marzo 1912.

en el puerto de Rosario, a cuyos componentes se les obtuvo carta de ciudadanía. Este grupo desfiló algunas veces, con su característica indumentaria, en las manifestaciones de la Liga del Sur.'

En un desfile liguista, en 1912, un militante radical provocó a la columna gritando: '¡E'viva Garibaldi! ¡E'viva Italia!'. La multitud de italianos que integraba el desfile, desconocedora del origen del grito, lo coreó entusiastamente. Una vez aclarada la situación, el radical tuvo que huir de las furias de los liguistas.[60] Los radicales también acusaban a la Liga de que uno de sus pilares, el gremio de almaceneros minoristas, mayoritariamente italiano, se dedicaba a la compra de libretas electorales, muchas veces a cambio de alcohol.[61]

Además de los extranjeros, la Liga encontró apoyo social entre los pequeños y medianos campesinos. Estos vínculos se vieron reflejados en el proyecto de ley presentado por de la Torre, sobre subdivisión de la tierra para fomento y colonización. La ley, según *La Capital*:

'Contribuirá a radicar al colono, haciéndolo propietario de la tierra que cultiva, con grandes facilidades de pago, y sin exigirle otra cosa más que sea trabajada por si mismo el área adquirida, de la que como es natural, ese agricultor tratará de sacar el mejor y el más abundante producto, con responsabilidades propias, y sin intermediarios de arrendamiento, pues entra en posesión de su solar desde el momento en que firma su compromiso con el gobierno provincial respectivo. En dicho proyecto se establece, que el gobierno nacional proporcionará a cada gobierno de provincia una suma determinada de millones de pesos con el fin de que compren tierras agrícolas en buenas condiciones por su situación y calidad, las que han de ser vendidas a precio justo y a largo plazo. También se propone la subdivisión de los grandes latifundios.'[62]

De acuerdo con el propio de la Torre, sin embargo, la Liga contaba entre sus adherentes a gente de todo el espectro social:

'Contamos con la mayoría de estancieros, chacareros, la gran mayoría de las firmas comerciales de Rosario, y de los pueblos vecinos, así como los operarios de la ciudad y la campaña.'[63]

Junto a los elementos modernizadores de la Liga, permanecían por lo demás algunos elementos antiguos. Así caracterizaba a la Liga una especie de

---

[60] Caballero, *Hipólito Yrigoyen*, p. 138-9.

[61] Caballero, *Hipólito Yrigoyen*, p. 142.

[62] *La Capital* (Rosario), 1 noviembre 1913.

[63] *La Capital*, 6 agosto 1910.

'corporativismo'. Por ejemplo, en la Cuarta Convención Electoral se aceptó un representante del Centro de Almaceneros y otros del gremio de Ingenieros, Arquitectos y Constructores, tal como era costumbre en el partido.[64] Para de la Torre, la Liga no era un partido político,

> 'pues entre sus miembros los había de diferentes credos a este respecto. El objeto de la Liga es el cumplimiento de la Constitución y las reformas necesarias que impongan las necesidades y el progreso de la Provincia'.[65]

En esta negativa a considerar a su agrupación como un partido político deben buscarse las razones del nombre adoptado por el organismo: Liga del Sur. En aquel entonces, había ligas de todo tipo presentes en múltiples actividades de la vida pública nacional.

Sin embargo, estaba claro, que más allá del rechazo a la concepción tradicional de los partidos políticos, de la Torre se había empeñado en crear una organización nueva, importando modelos de los Estados Unidos y poniendo el acento de la diferencia en la existencia de un programa político explícito y detallado, única forma de superar los personalismos y los caudillismos que habían caracterizado hasta entonces a la 'política criolla'. De este modo, la Liga del Sur se convirtió en un referente de la vida política santafesina y muy pronto comenzó a tener una significación nacional, especialmente a partir de la reforma electoral de Roque Sáenz Peña. La presencia de Lisandro de la Torre en el parlamento nacional sirvió para proyectar su modelo de partido más allá de los estrechos límites de su provincia natal y para plantear la posibilidad, luego fracasada, de construir a imagen y semejanza de la Liga del Sur un gran partido político nacional que pudiera enfrentarse exitosamente al peligro populista expresado por el radicalismo yrigoyenista.

---

[64] *La Capital*, 5 noviembre 1912.

[65] *La Capital*, 6 agosto 1910.

CHAPTER 5

Nationalism and State-Building in Latin American History

D. A. Brading

I

Nationalism is an ideology which purports to sanction and legitimise the existence of nation-states. According to Ernest Gellner, it is an offspring of modernisation.[1] The Industrial Revolution unleashed a process of continuous economic change, an historic cycle now two hundred years old, which slowly but inevitably has brought dense urbanisation and some measure of industrialisation to most countries of the world. Parallel to this process, both state and industry have invested resources to create communication networks, based on universal education and the media, which in turn generally diffuse a common language and common cultural values. Peasants do not merely become workers, they and their children become citizens, proud members of nation-states. To strengthen social solidarity the communal values of folk culture are re-stated within a national context so that the intrinsic qualities of the local language, the achievements of literature both popular and aristocratic, and the glorious deeds of ancestral heroes, all become articles of a patriot creed. It is the task of intellectuals to articulate the nascent consciousness of new nation-states. In all this, as Gellner insists, there is a paradox. For the invocation of historical and literary achievements masks the modernisation process whereby nation-states are integrated into the international framework of industrial society. Moreover, virtually all students of nationalism agree that there is little that is necessary or inevitable about the existence or identity of any given nation state. As Benedict Anderson has argued, nations are imaginary communities: their existence depends on the conscious affirmation of a people that they constitute a nation and thereby differ from their neighbours.[2] Nationalism is thus an ideology which defines both the intrinsic and differential basis of identity. In this context it is useful to recall Ernest Renan's famous lecture, 'What is a Nation?', delivered in 1882 at the Sorbonne, where he argued that the 'historic individualities' of Western nations could not be explained by the determinants of race, language, religion, economics and geography, since exceptions to all these elements could be found. Instead, he declared that 'a nation is a living soul, a spiritual principle.... a moral consciousness', which was defined by 'the common possession of a rich heritage of memories' and was animated by

---

[1] Ernest Gellner, *Nations and Nationalism* (Oxford, 1983), pp. 1-7, 37-52, 124-6.

[2] Benedict Anderson, *Imagined Communities: Reflections on the Origin and Spread of Nationalism* (London, 1983), *passim*; Gellner, *Nations and Nationalism*, pp. 53-61.

'current consent, the desire to live together, the will to preserve worthily the individual inheritance which has been handed down'. It was a community built upon past experience and sustained by present agreement. If 'a heroic past, great men, glory.... form the social capital, upon which a national idea may be founded' the current, living nation formed 'a great solidarity', its existence ratified by 'a daily plebiscite'. Renan concluded by citing the hymn chanted by young Spartan warriors to their elders : 'We are what you were; we shall become what you are'.[3]

The fountainhead of nationalist ideology was German philosophic idealism. It was a creed formulated by intellectuals drawn from the middle ranks of society who rejected the aristocratic culture of the German courts which was then dominated by French language and literature. The universal values of the Enlightenment were replaced by an appeal to history and the particular values of the nation. Thinkers such as Herder, Fichte and the romantics laid the philosophic foundations for a nationalism which asserted that the individual was shaped, if not determined, by membership of a social group and that the primary social group was not the family, the city or the church, but the nation. Moreover, each nation was thought to be an organic entity, animated by a collective spirit whose particular character could be discerned in its language, literature, arts, laws and institutions, all articulated across history. Not merely did each nation possess its own specific values and interests, but these values and interests had priority over the universal goals of religion, empires, economics and political philosophy.[4] The application of nationalist ideology to practical concerns can be best observed in Fichte's celebrated *Addresses to the German Nation* (1807-8), delivered in Berlin after Napoleon's defeat of Prussia and Austria. Influenced by Schiller's prophetic thesis, that the third age of humanity was about to dawn, when beauty and freedom would command the world, he summoned German youth to initiate the grand task of creating a new, more vital culture. Only through education could a new German nation be formed. Since the cities were the home of culture it was important to protect their prosperity by rendering them independent of foreign industry and trade. All these measures were more important than any exercise in state building. The resurgent character of this rhetoric was most evident in Fichte's assertion that German was the only truly living language in Europe, constantly renewing its vitality by return to its roots, a quality which distinguished it from the abstract, artificial nature of the Romance tongues. He concluded by prophesying that Germany was destined to become 'the regenerator and re-creator of the world'.[5] It was in Russia during the 1840s that German romantic nationalism was first appropriated and given

---

[3]   Ernest Renan, *The Poetry of the Celtic Races and Other Studies* (London, 1896), pp. 61-83.

[4]   Isaiah Berlin, *Against the Current. Essays in the History of Ideas* (London, 1979), pp. 333-55; see also, A.D. Smith, *Theories of Nationalism*, 2nd. edn. (London, 1983), pp. 27-40; and Elie Kedourie, *Nationalism* (London, 1960), *passim*.

[5]   J.H. Fichte, *Addresses to the German Nation* (Chicago, 1922), pp. 68-9, 102-3, 253-5.

local application. There, the Tsarist regime maintained a great multi-ethnic, bureaucratic empire sustained by the nobility, church and army, and justified by the principles of orthodoxy, autocracy and nationality. It was sharply criticised by the Westernisers, liberal intellectuals who advocated the introduction of European forms of representative government and individual rights. But the Westernisers were attacked by the Slavophiles who defended the Orthodox Church, idealised the medieval past, and affirmed that Russian social values were best maintained in the peasant commune. In politics these gentry intellectuals advocated the principle of conciliation, an ill-defined process whereby the Tsar would retain absolute authority, but extend its scope by extensive consultation and the achievement of consensus. Disdainful of Western individualism and the spiritual vacuum they discerned in the current obsession with economic progress, the Slavophiles echoed and applied Fichte's vision, prophesying that Holy Russia would one day emerge as the spiritual regenerator of mankind.[6]

In Spain it was the Generation of 1898 who invoked the principles of romantic nationalism to revive a country defeated by the United States. They lived in an epoch when Spain's economy was experiencing significant modernisation and when Spanish culture was dominated by French masters. In *En torno al casticismo* (1894-1911), Miguel de Unamuno addressed himself to the youth of his country, confident that the 'alma común....el espíritu colectivo' of the Spanish people would overcome the current 'marasmo', the inert atomism that still plagued it, striving once more to express its enduring values in new works of literature and art. He denounced the 'europeanisation' of Spain and insisted on its 'intrahistory', which was to say, the *castizo* spirit which had been shaped by the interaction of man and nature on the harsh plains of Castile, a centuries-long process in which the race which still constituted the nucleus of Spanish nationality had been formed. To this day, the character of the nation and its language were best observed amidst the peasantry of Castile.[7] The defensive quality of this nationalist rhetoric was most clearly expressed by Unamuno in his essay entitled 'Sobre la Europeización', in which he confessed to 'an inner repugnance' to 'the governing principles of the modern European spirit, to the scientific orthodoxy of today...' In this distaste for science, so he averred, Unamuno was representative of the Spanish people who by reason of their preoccupation with religion and death still hesitated to accept Western utilitarian philosophy and economics. More particularly, Unamuno denounced French as the language of logic and mediocrity, the expression of a people who lacked passion, had never nurtured great mystics, and to whom the spiritual depths of Spain were simply unimaginable. As exemplars to inspire the young generation Unamuno invoked the heroic achievements of the sixteenth and seventeenth

---

[6]   Martin Malia, *Alexander Herzen and the Birth of Russian Socialism* (New York, 1965), pp. 278-334.

[7]   Miguel de Unamuno, *En torno al casticismo* (Madrid, 1943), pp. 28, 54-6, 102-13, 130-41.

centuries when the *castizo* spirit of the nation had found its purest articulation in the life and works of San Juan de la Cruz. It was now time for the Spanish people to return to 'our old African wisdom, to our popular wisdom', refraining henceforth from imitating foreign models, and thereby revive ancestral values.[8] Unlike his German and Russian predecessors, however, Unamuno appears not to have fixed upon any world-regeneration role for Spain and its people.

To emphasise the ideological character of nationalism is not to deny that it is also a form of politics. As John Breuilly has argued, nationalist rhetoric has been constantly deployed by political leaders to mobilise the masses and thereby achieve power.[9] The great empires of the nineteenth and early twentieth centuries were generally multi-national and although they relied on provincial elites to maintain their authority, they usually confined the upper echelons of the bureaucracy to individuals of the dominant nation. These polities often survived by inertia, since any attempt to strengthen the power and presence of the imperial bureaucracy tended to exclude and hence alienate the provincial elites.[10] In effect, nationalist ideology provided separatist leaders with the arguments and rhetoric to stir the masses and to justify independence. There was a paradox, however, in this process whereby nascent nations obtained recognition as independent states. As John Breuilly has observed, the right of peoples to choose their own form of government and hence free themselves from imperial rule depends on the existence of an international community which accepts the liberal tenets of popular sovereignty and representative government and individual rights.[11] It was the American and still more the French Revolution which heralded the emergence of this new world order, their principles endowed with universal application by Woodrow Wilson at Versailles. Nationalism thus offered intellectuals and politicians the ideological instruments with which to identify the nation, to demonstrate its historic existence and enduring character; but it cannot construe acceptable arguments for the right to self government. The achievement of state sovereignty depends on international recognition and hence can only be justified by doctrines taken from international law or the tenets of liberalism.

.Finally, it should be emphasised that nationalism was preceded and paralleled by classical republicanism, a doctrine which derived from the civic humanism of Renaissance Florence and found political expression during the French Revolution. Associated with liberalism, it was logically distinct, since republican doctrine affirmed that man was essentially a political animal who found fulfilment as a citizen of a free republic, achieving glory in its service,

---

[8]   Miguel de Unamuno, *Ensayos*, 7 vols. (Madrid, 1918), Vol. VII, pp. 186-91, 221-49.

[9]   John Breuilly, *Nationalism and the State* (Manchester, 1982), pp. 186-91, 221-49.

[10]   Smith, *Theories of Nationalism*, pp. 231-51.

[11]   Breuilly, *Nationalism and the State* , pp. 60-2, 352-73.

always ready to sacrifice his life in defence of the *patria*.[12] If romantic nationalists found inspiration in Gothic chivalry and medieval epics, republicans always cited the heroes of ancient Greece and Rome. There was a universal creed in which each *patria* was conceived as possessing much the same institutions and laws, all inspired by classical precedent. In effect German romantic nationalism and French neoclassic republicanism flourished in Europe at much the same time: both were profoundly historicist, scanning the past for heroes, art forms and moral values; both exhorted citizens to serve and die for their countries; and both, through journalism and education, directed their message to the masses, seeking to inculcate loyalty to the nation state, no matter what its ostensible form of government.[13]

It is the thesis of this paper that in Latin America, nationalism was a late-comer, a child of the twentieth century. The reasons for this retardation are relatively obvious. When the Spanish empire dissolved, the republics which inherited its domain justified their separation from the metropolis by doctrines borrowed from the American and French Revolutions. Boundaries were determined by former provincial jurisdictions or by civil war: there was no question of national identity justifying any particular state's existence. Moreover, when central governments consolidated their authority during the middle decades of the nineteenth century, their leaders invoked a blend of liberal and republican discourse, usually taken from French sources. The very cult of patriotic heroes, so common in this epoch, only served to strengthen the diffusion of neo-classical republicanism. Nor did the arrival of Comptean positivism weaken its hegemony. In effect, it was only at the start of the twentieth century that romantic idealism, still often mediated through French authors, actively entered the region, there to inspire almost immediately the first stirrings and pronouncements of nationalism. Within three decades an entire library of books and pamphlets on national themes had been composed. But as yet we entirely lack any systematic analysis of their content or provenance, even at the level of particular countries.[14] At the same time, this literary outburst was accompanied by an ever more powerful process of economic modernisation and state-building based on popular mobilisation. Nationalist ideology thus served to justify and legitimise often authoritarian regimes which deployed state power to transform the economy and create national identity. The correlation of nationalism and state-building, however, was not always exact, and at times the two phenomena existed in separate compartments, unable to find common ground.

---

[12] J.G.A. Pocock, *The Machiavellian Moment: Florentine Political Thought and the Atlantic Republican Tradition* (Princeton, 1975), pp. 48-82, 165-219.

[13] Robert Rosenblum, *Transformations in Late Eighteenth Century Art* (Princeton, 1967) pp. 47-9, 70-2; Robert L. Herbert, *David, Voltaire, Brutus and the French Revolution* (London, 1972), pp. 70-1, 109.

[14] Few of the books dealing with nationalism even mention Latin America.

II

The movement for independence in Spanish America was caused by the Creole elite's resentment at 'the revolution in government' implemented by the enlightened ministers of Carlos II (1759-88). Inspired by the principles of enlightened despotism, the Bourbon kings re-built the colonial state, introducing a salaried fiscal bureaucracy and small standing armies in all the chief provinces of the American empire. At the same time, reforms in the structure of trade and taxation promoted a dramatic expansion in the export economy based on soaring output of precious metals and tropical crops. The success of these measures was registered in the revival of Spanish naval and military power, allowing the monarchy once more to play a significant role in the European concert. For the Creole elite, however, the growing prosperity of the American empire was but poor compensation for their renewed exclusion from high office in Church and State. The official places created by the revolution in government mainly went to Peninsular Spaniards; the fiscal profit accruing from the economic expansion swelled the monarchy's coffers in Spain.[15] The result was that, when news of the American and French Revolutions slowly became known, educated Creoles began to consider the possibility of independence. When Napoleon in 1810 deposed the Bourbons and installed his brother Joseph as king of Spain, thereby provoking mass rebellion across the Peninsula, the Creole elite in virtually all the provincial capitals of the American empire demanded the convocation of representative juntas, demands that soon prompted either the seizure of power or a conservative reaction by the colonial authorities. The imperial crisis deepened in 1812, when the Cortes of Cádiz promulgated a constitution which vested sovereignty in the Spanish people and converted the monarchy into an hereditary executive, since conservative Creoles affirmed their loyalty to the king, but resented Peninsular officials in America, and abhorred any subjection to the Spanish people.[16]

But on what grounds could the American Spaniards justify rupture from Spain? In the first instance, Creole city councils and juntas simply argued that with the Bourbon abdication sovereignty returned to the people. Each major province of the empire formed a kingdom in itself, endowed with all the institutions necessary for self government. Such arguments, however, simply placed Mexico and Peru on the same footing as Andalucía and Aragón. To justify independence, the Creoles asserted that Spain had installed a tyrannical regime in the New World which exploited its subjects and excluded them from any participation in government. As Simón Bolívar exclaimed : 'We were never

---

[15] D.A. Brading, *Miners and Merchants in Bourbon Mexico 1763-1810* (Cambridge, 1971), pp. 19-56.

[16] D.A. Brading, *The First America: The Spanish Monarchy, Creole Patriots and the Liberal State 1492-1867* (Cambridge, 1991), pp. 535-60.

viceroys nor governors ... seldom archbishops and bishops; never diplomats; soldiers only in subordinate rank; nobles without privileges; in effect, we were never magistrates, nor financiers and rarely even merchants'. Invoking Montesquieu's concept of oriental despotism, Bolívar claimed that the Spanish empire was even more oppressive than its counterparts in Turkey and Persia, since in those countries the monarchs at least employed native ministers. The 'active tyranny' of Spain had reduced the Creoles to perpetual infancy, their worldly action confined to the economic sphere, acting as mere producers and consumers of commodities, forever denied that participation in politics which was the prerogative of the free citizen.[17] In effect, Bolívar here expressed the classical republican doctrine that men can only find fulfilment of their moral powers as citizens of free republics, pursuing glory in politics, warfare and the arts, all undertaken in service of their *patria*.

If separation from Spain could thus be based on arguments which echoed the doctrines of the American and French Revolutions, problems immediately arose when the Creoles sought to delineate the boundaries of the successor states. Barely had they become conscious of their identity as *Americanos*, as distinct from *Españoles Americanos*, than they were obliged to proclaim themselves Colombianos, Bolivianos and Mexicanos. Yet Creoles of Lima and Mexico differed from each other little more than the inhabitants of Seville and Valladolid. Although rebel leaders sought to preserve the boundaries of the old colonial jurisdictions, invoking the principle of *uti possidetis*, provincial rivalries soon threatened the very existence of the new republics. The junta at Buenos Aires demanded obedience from all the inhabitants of the vast viceroyalty of La Plata, only soon to encounter its authority repudiated by leaders of Uruguay and Paraguay. Thereafter, the governors of the interior states organised their own militia and exercised autonomous power. Much the same process of dissolution occurred in Central America where the first republic fell prey to civil war and during the 1840s divided into five separate republics. Although Simón Bolívar created the republic of Colombia to administer the territories of the viceroyalty of New Granada and later projected a pan-Andean federation to unite Colombia and Peru, his state building exercises all failed. In 1830 Venezuela, New Granada and Ecuador all went their separate ways. Moreover it was not until the 1840s, after two attempts at federation and conquest had failed, that Peru and Bolivia agreed to respect their mutual independence. Only Mexico succeeded in maintaining the boundaries of the former viceroyalty and indeed, thanks to Chiapas joining the federation, actually augmented its territory, an achievement, however, soon to be overshadowed by the US annexation of the vast provinces lying to the north of the Rio Grande. In effect, the territorial identity of the new republics was often arbitrary, usually contested by neighbours, and was simply based on colonial precedent.

---

[17] *Ibid.*, pp. 603-20; Simón Bolívar, *Obras completas*, ed. Vicente Lecuna, 3 vols. (Caracas, 1964), vol I, pp. 159-86.

To achieve independence, it was necessary for disaffected Creoles to mobilise the masses, a tactic which often prompted swift conservative reaction, thereby transforming the rebellion into civil war. The problem here was that in both country and city the masses comprised indians, mestizos, blacks, mulattos and poor whites whose ethnic *calidad* had been carefully maintained by both Church and State. To attract support, Creoles now proclaimed the end of all racial distinctions. As José María Morelos, the Mexican insurgent leader, declared : 'with the exception of the Europeans, henceforth all the population shall not be named according to their *calidad* as indians, mulattos or other castes, but all generally as Americans'.[18] But the dangers of race warfare, which was to say, the danger that the coloured masses might seek to exterminate the white elite, imitating events in Haiti, haunted Simón Bolívar and he adopted harsh measures to avert the threat. The persistence and prevalence of ethnic hierarchy thus made nonsense of any presumption of nationality or nationhood in Spanish America. When Bolívar framed a constitution for Bolivia, he disenfranchised all illiterates, reducing the body of active citizens to minuscule proportions.[19]

To emphasise the immense difficulties confronting any attempt to create a series of nation-states from the break-up of the Spanish empire, is not to deny the strength of Creole attachment to their respective *patrias*, a concept which had come to embrace entire provinces as well as cities. From the early seventeenth century Creole chroniclers and preachers had celebrated the talents and achievements of their 'nation' and the glories of their *patria*. In New Spain the cult of Our Lady of Guadalupe had acquired strong patriotic significance, especially when in 1746 the Mexican virgin was acclaimed as common patron of all the dioceses of New Spain. In 1810 Miguel Hidalgo, the insurgent leader, offered his followers her image as their banner, thereby seeking to strengthen and legitimise his movement by appeal to religious sentiments. At the same time, insurgent ideologues such as Fray Servando de Mier and Carlos María de Bustamante drew upon Creole chroniclers to install the Aztec empire as foundation of Mexican history, portraying the insurgency as a struggle to recover the independence which the Mexican nation had lost during the Spanish conquest. So persuasive were their arguments that the 1821 Act of Independence, framed by former royalists, proclaimed : 'The Mexican nation, which for three hundred years has had neither its own will nor free use of its voice, today leaves the oppression in which it has lived.' Only in Mexico did Creole patriotism flower into a form of insurgent nationalism, which no matter how precocious or premature, drew upon sentiments and arguments that were in part reiterated during the twentieth century.[20] That it was tied to an equally strong republicanism makes the case all the more interesting.

---

[18]   Ernesto Lemoine Villacaña, *Morelos* (Mexico, 1965), pp. 162, 181, 264.

[19]   A contemporary English translation of this constitution can be found in John Miller, *Memoirs of General Miller*, 2 vols. (London, 1828), Vol. II, pp. 372-439.

[20]   Brading, *The First America*, pp. 561-602.

That the civil wars which accompanied the struggle for independence were swiftly followed by military coups and political disintegration meant that the new republics lacked legitimacy. The paper constitutions devised by liberal lawyers commanded little respect and were soon discarded. The result was instability that verged on anarchy. As Lorenzo de Zavala, a Mexican radical observed: 'In a young nation, shaken by continual violence, where along with the chains which once oppressed it, there have also disappeared the old bonds of subordination, a good part of the former habits of order, and to a certain extent the very common interests which should sustain it...'[21] For Simón Bolívar, who wrote a despondent survey of the hemisphere in 1829, Spanish America resembled Europe after the fall of the Roman empire, caught in a new Dark Age, in which the new republics had already disintegrated into petty fiefdoms and factious city-states, a condition which led him to prophesy : 'this country will infallibly fall into the hands of uncontrollable multitudes, thereafter to pass to almost imperceptible tyrants of all colours and races'.[22] His statement certainly applied to Venezuela and Argentina where power was exercised by local caudillos, leaders recruited from landowners or militia captains, who enjoyed a personal ascendency based on control of the local means of violence. By contrast, in Mexico and Peru the officers of the former royalist armies maintained or re-constituted their forces and thereafter governed these countries until the middle decades of the century, their internal competition for political power the cause of incessant coups and conflict.[23] Throughout the continent there was enacted a gradual process whereby local elites and their chosen leaders slowly constructed networks of authority, based on violence, kinship, property and common interests. In these circumstances the task of central government was to govern the capital city and its hinterland, mediate between competing caudillos, and manage foreign affairs so as to avoid foreign intervention. The grand absentee in this cycle of violence and tyranny was any sense of nationhood.

It fell to the generation of leaders who seized power in the 1850s, the generation of Benito Juárez and Bartolomé Mitre, to rebuild the authority of the central government. In both Mexico and Argentina presidents appeared, recruited from the Liberal camp, who succeeded in forging broad coalitions which enabled them to re-establish internal peace and strengthen central government, thereby creating the conditions for economic progress. In both cases the emergence of a regular army, led by officers loyal to the president, was indispensable since it allowed the government once more to exercise that monopoly over violence which Max Weber defined as the hall-mark of the

---

[21]   Lorenzo de Zavala, *Ensayo crítico de las revoluciones de México desde 1808 hasta 1830*, 2 vols. (Mexico, 1918), Vol. II, p. 301.

[22]   Bolívar, *Obras*, Vol. III, pp. 841-7.

[23]   Celia Wu, *Generals and Diplomats. Great Britain and Peru 1820-40* (Cambridge, 1991), pp. 11-33.

modern state. But if the more egregious caudillos were soon eliminated, their role in provincial politics was assumed by state governors generally recruited from the local landowning elite. As Francisco Bulnes observed: 'the effective force of the Mexican Liberal party has always been the *caciques*'. At the same time, he recognised that Juárez's long tenure as president, when combined with his successful resistance to the French intervention, had enabled him to re-build the prestige and authority of his office. He concluded by describing Juárez as 'a secular Zapotec Buddha' whose apotheosis as a national hero derived from the residual Catholicism of the Mexican people, 'which always looks for an image, a cult, a piety for social emotions'.[24]

In the sphere of ideology, the regimes which re-established the authority of central government exhibited a dichotomy verging on schizo-phrenia, between what their leaders said and what their leaders did. The political reality was presidential autocracy or parliamentary oligarchy sustained by local caciques and the regular army, with ballots rigged and elections a mere formality. Yet the political rhetoric which justified these regimes invoked the doctrines of classical republicanism. In particular, the cult of patriotic heroes offered politicians ample occasion for public celebration and commemoration of republican virtue. A civic liturgy was devised, replete with its calendar of feasts and anniversaries, its monuments and statues, and its public ritual. The first president of a united Argentina, Bartolomé Mitre, composed laudatory biographies of Manuel Belgrano and José de San Martín, installing the Buenos Aires 1810 revolution and junta as the founding moment of the new republic.[25] So too, in Mexico the radical intellectuals Ignacio Ramírez and Ignacio Manuel Altamirano hailed Miguel Hidalgo as the founding father of their liberal *patria*, thereby presenting the 1810 insurgency as the popular precedent of the Reforma. It fell to their disciple, Justo Sierra, to write the life of Juárez, in which, drawing upon Carlyle's description of Cromwell, he lauded the president as a silent hero who discerned and expressed the inner will of his country and people far better than any man of ideas or words.[26] In short, as the nineteenth century drew to a close, almost every republic in Spanish America had devised its own *historia patria*, texts which formed generations of schoolchildren and offered politicians material for their speeches, wherein both founding fathers and subsequent leaders were celebrated as models of public virtue, worthy of emulation by all citizens. In ideology the French example thus reigned supreme, the very alternation of Bonapartist and republican rhetoric evoking a resonant response, based on a presumed similarity of political experience.

---

[24] Cited in Brading, *The First America*, pp. 665-6.

[25] Germán Colmenares, *Las convenciones contra la cultura. Ensayos sobre la historiografía hispanoamericana del siglo XIX* (Bogotá, 1987), pp. 137-63.

[26] Brading, *The First America*, pp. 665-8.

III

It was at the very start of the twentieth century that romantic nationalism at last appeared in Latin America. By then the hemisphere was engulfed in a dramatic expansion in the export economy, sustained by massive foreign investment, and accompanied by rapid growth of population in ports and capital cities. The urban middle class provided a new audience for newspapers and reviews. But the greater ease of travel and communication effected by industrial advance also brought home to Spanish American statesmen and intellectuals the overwhelming economic progress of the United States, then experiencing industrialisation on a scale unimaginable to its Latin neighbours. This concentration of power and riches became positively threatening when the United States easily defeated Spain in 1898, annexed Puerto Rico and the Philippines, established a protectorate over Cuba, and thereafter engineered Panama's independence so as to obtain control over the Canal Zone. The Anglo-US colossus was thus portrayed as both the embodiment of Western progress and as a political threat to Spanish American freedom. It was in this context of rapid internal modernisation and imperialist challenge that nationalist ideology found an enthusiastic audience throughout the hemisphere.

In *Ariel* (1900), José Enrique Rodó, a Uruguayan essayist, condemned the nineteenth century for its obsession with material progress and dominion over natural forces. It was an age which had enthroned Caliban, ushering in democracy and elevating mediocrity as the human norm, so that all distinctions or heroic achievements were derided. Already, thinkers as diverse as Comte, Taine and Renan had warned of the dangers of democracy and 'the great voice of Carlyle' had celebrated the role of heroes in history. It was now time for the youth of Spanish America to adopt the role of Ariel and to strive for the rebirth of reason, of beauty, and of the spirit, ensuring that the man of superior talent, the natural aristocracy, would effectively govern and lead the masses, no matter what the political system. This high flown appeal might not have attracted so much attention had not Rodó defined the United States as the very embodiment of the utilitarian, democratic spirit, defining it as 'a school of will-power and work', where truth and beauty were disdained and taste and sensibility notable only for their absence. It was a country dominated by a vulgar plutocracy, caught up in a cycle of incessant toil and change, bereft of any capacity for aesthetic contemplation. None of this was cause for alarm had not many Spanish Americans sought to imitate the United States, their cultural tradition undermined by 'nordomania' . At the same time, Spanish America was threatened by the democratic degeneration caused by mass immigration from Europe, a phenomenon all too obvious in Argentina and Uruguay, which threatened to reduce the great cities of the zone into mere commercial emporia. Yet Latin America had once bred a generation of generals, poets and heroes who had fought for independence and thereafter created the republics. 'We Latin

Americans have a racial inheritance, a great ethnic tradition' which the young intellectuals had to preserve and revive.[27]

If Rodó elicited such widespread enthusiasm, it was in part because he refrained from applying his ideas to practical politics. A native of Uruguay, the son of immigrant parents, he eschewed any narrow patriotism, exclaiming that 'for the hispano-americans the *patria* is Spanish America'. On welcoming the appearance of romantic literature and ideals, he surmised that their adoption would promote national literature and thereby assist the nation 'to form and develop its collective personality, its own genius, the Hispanic American soul'. Unlike Unamuno, however, Rodó idolised France as the embodiment of the Latin spirit, stating: 'when we talk of France we cannot talk as foreigners.....we see in her the supreme flowering of the Latin spirit, which flies across the centuries and the world, maintaining the august lessons of disinterested idealism against overweening force and utilitarian incentives'. Closer to home, he fixed upon Simón Bolívar as the key figure in Spanish American history, hailing him as an aristocratic Alcibiades who was both a great captain and a prophetic intellectual, 'the clay of America fired by the breath of genius'. Above all, he saluted Bolívar as the advocate of Spanish American confederation, even if he admitted that 'the political unity which consecrates and embodies the moral unity – Bolívar's dream – is still a dream, which the present generation will perhaps not see realised'.[28] In short, Rodó was a cultural nationalist who identified all Spanish America as his *patria* and nation.

To observe the political application of these doctrines, we have only to explore the career of José Vasconcelos, who in 1921 became first rector of the National University of Mexico and then minister of education. In his inaugural address as rector, he announced that he spoke as the 'delegate of the Revolution', calling upon the university to work on behalf of the Mexican people, assisting the masses to escape from their poverty and ignorance. 'The Revolution now walks in search of scholars....let us become the initiators of a crusade in public education.' Equally important, he stated that 'it is the responsibility of the national university to define the character of Mexican culture' and gave that institution the heraldic inscription it still employs: 'by my race the spirit will speak'.[29] As minister, Vasconcelos despatched rural missions to promote popular education, established agricultural research stations, engineering schools and public libraries, and created a network of cultural institutions that still survive. It was thanks to his patronage and inspiration that an entire generation of young intellectuals and artists entered public service, among them the great muralists Diego Rivera and José Clemente Orozco. In

[27] José Enrique Rodó, *Ariel, Liberalismo y Jacobinismo* (Montevideo, 1964), pp. 36-40, 45, 57-62, 83-8.

[28] José Enrique Rodó, *Obras completas* (Buenos Aires, 1958), pp. 574-5, 747, 760, 772.

[29] José Vasconcelos, *Obras completas*, 4 vols. (Mexico, 1961), Vol. II. pp. 773, 775, 781.

effect, Vasconcelos conceived of education and culture as the instruments of nation-building, the means of incorporating the peasantry and urban workers into the nation. In a speech delivered in Brazil, he proclaimed that it was now time for Latin America to achieve its second independence, 'an independence in civilisation, an emancipation of the spirit'. He characterised the nineteenth century as 'an apish period', when slavish imitation of foreign models, especially of France, had reduced Latin America to the condition of 'spiritual colonies'. But now, so he claimed, he heard 'the voices of a great race which begins to dance in the light'.[30]

In *La Raza Cósmica* (1925) and *Indología* (1926), works published after his resignation from government, Vasconcelos developed his nationalist ideology to an appropriate messianic conclusion. In his reading he had abandoned the French authors favoured by Rodó to engage directly with Schopenhauer, Nietzsche and other German philosophers. It was presumably from Schiller's *Letters on the Authentic Education of Man* that he derived his division of human history into three great stages, in which the first age, the military or material phase was dominated by mere force; the second, the intellectual or material phase was governed by science and law, and hence formed an epoch of competition between nation-states; and the third, the aesthetic or spiritual age, was animated by love and beauty, and hence was a period of confederations and peace. But Vasconcelos gave these familiar doctrines an original application when he declared that the New World was to be the predestined scene where the third age would blossom. After all, Europe and Asia were decrepit and Africa immature. As was to be expected, the United States did not figure in this pleasing prospect, since its current success demonstrated that it belonged to the second stage of history, the age of industry, science and competition. In short, it was Hispanic America, both Portuguese and Spanish, which was about to enter its epoch of manifest destiny. In all this, the child of promise, the chosen race, was the mestizo. Scornfully dismissing the theories of Herbert Spencer and Gustave le Bon about the instability or degeneracy of hybrid nations as mere imperialist slander, Vasconcelos proclaimed that the mestizos formed the fifth great race of humanity, as a universal synthesis, the culminating blend of the peoples of Europe, Africa, Asia and America. In culture hispanic or Latin, this race had already displayed its peculiar aptitude for aesthetic creation and erotic activity, thereby offering a fitting prelude for the future reign of love and beauty.[31] What is striking about these messianic projections is that Vasconcelos had so little to say about the character or destiny of Mexico and its nation, his romantic nationalism encompassing the entire Hispanic American race.

---

[30] *Ibid.,* Vol. II, pp. 851-2.

[31] *Ibid.,* Vol. II, pp. 903-1280; see also D. A. Brading, *Prophecy and Myth in Mexican History* (Cambridge, 1984), pp. 71-8.

The transition from literary romanticism to state-building and economic nationalism can be clearly observed in the career of Manuel Ugarte, an Argentine intellectual of the Generation of 1900, who in a plethora of books and lecture tours across the hemisphere, actively preached the necessity of Spanish American unity. As much as Rodó, a personal friend, he identified with the *patria grande* as the only bulwark against the encroachments of the United States. In literature he hailed José Hernández's gaucho epic, *Martín Fierro*, only then to lament that it had found no successors. Yet despite this nostalgia for rural society, he also insisted on economic modernisation. Obsessed with the expansion of US investment and corporations into Latin America, which threatened to reduce its republics to the condition of mere colonies, he denounced the feudal backwardness of 'Iberian civilisation', the result, so he argued, of chronic political divisions and false cultural ideals. As early as 1915, he advocated the nationalisation of the British-owned railways in Argentina and the creation of a national industry which would liberate the country from its current dependence on primary exports. By then he had already broken with the Socialist party, of which he was member for many years, for its failure to confront Argentine problems and its dogmatic Marxism. On being attacked for his 'nacionalismo criollo', he affirmed his belief in the army, in the preservation of private property, of respect for religion, and above all, in the *patria*. It was necessary for the state to intervene in the economic sphere, acting both to promote economic development and to ensure a just distribution of income. With this kind of programme in mind, it was perhaps inevitable that Ugarte should have applauded the advent of Juan Domingo Perón, recounting with pride his interview with the new president, whom he counselled to inaugurate at once the construction of heavy industry in Argentina. Oh leaving the national palace, he exclaimed: 'We have a great president'.[32] In effect, Ugarte was but one of an entire generation of Argentine intellectuals to embrace the nationalist cause, their diverse ideas and options combining to form a climate of opinion in which Peronism was to thrive. The degree to which nationalism was a form of practical politics which fought both North American imperialism and Marxist ideology was most obviously demonstrated in the foundation of the Apra party of Peru. In *El antimperialismo y el Apra* (1928), Víctor Raúl Haya de la Torre argued that the chief danger to Indoamerica came from the United States, which had but recently despatched troops to occupy several countries in Central America and the Caribbean and which threatened to reduce the entire region to a mere economic dependency. Indeed, local governments only exercised such authority as the imperialist powers allowed them. The challenge to independence was rendered all the more acute by the virtual treason of the governing class, composed of great landowners and their political agents, which acted as imperialism's fifth column all too prone to sell national resources to foreign investors in return for personal profit. To counter this sinister alliance, Haya de la Torre sought to form a mass political movement, a broad coalition of the middle classes with peasants and workers. It was a proposal which brought Haya

---

[32] Manuel Ugarte, *La nación latinoamericana*, ed. Norberto Galasso (Caracas, 1978), pp. 71-8.

de la Torre into direct confrontation with the nascent communist party and with José Mariátegui, the leading Peruvian Marxist. Meeting their critique head-on, he accused Marxists of mechanically applying ideas and measures to American problems, thereby opting for dogma over analysis of reality. Whereas Lenin had defined imperialism as the last phase of capitalism, for Indoamerica it was the first phase of modernisation, since it had established an export economy in primary produce. As yet the industrial proletariat was minuscule and labourers employed by foreign-owned plantations and mines often received higher wages than before. The chief sufferers from the inroads of imperialism were thus not the working class but the middle class, which was to say, petty industrialists, merchants, miners and small landowners, who all had suffered the impact of foreign investment and competition. To defend 'national liberty', it was thus necessary to create a strong national state based on a broad political movement which embraced the middle classes, workers and peasants. An essential pre-requisite of any consolidation of power would be the destruction of the landowning oligarchy and the distribution of land to the Indian *ayllus*. Only then could the aims of 'Indoamerican economic nationalism' be implemented. To support his bold rejection of Marxist theory, Haya de la Torre cited the example of the Kuomintang in China and, more persuasively, the achievements of the Mexican Revolution, citing in particular articles 27 and 123 of the 1917 Constitution which established the legal foundations for agrarian reform and labour legislation. He concluded: 'in our countries the capitalist phase ought therefore to be introduced under the aegis of the anti-imperialist state'.[33]

As Aprista doctrine attests, the Mexican Revolution and the regime it generated afforded Latin America the spectacle of mass mobilisation, state-building and nationalist ideology, all slowly combining to form a unique political culture. In *Forjando Patria* (1916), Manuel Gamio, Mexico's foremost archaeologist, welcomed the Revolution for its destruction of obstacles to the creation of 'the future nationality....the future Mexican *patria*'. Judged by the standards of Germany, Japan and France, Mexico did not yet constitute a true nation, since it lacked the four defining features of a common language, a common character, a homogeneous race and a shared history. By reason of their several languages, poverty and illiteracy, the Indian communities formed a series of *pequeñas patrias* whose inhabitants did not participate in national life nor exercise their rights as citizens. The grand aim of the Revolution, Gamio argued, must be to create 'a powerful *patria* and a coherent defined nationality', based on 'racial approximation, cultural fusion, linguistic unification and economic equilibrium'.[34]

---

[33] Víctor Raúl Haya de la Torre, *El Antimperialismo y el Apra*, 2nd edn. (Santiago de Chile, 1936), pp. 18-21, 64-9, 82-7, 133-6, 159.

[34] Manuel Gamio, *Forjando patria*, 2nd. edn. (Mexico, 1960), pp. 6-8, 12, 183.

As Director of the newly founded Department of Anthropology and Archaeology, Gamio assembled a numerous team of experts, recruited from several disciplines, both to excavate and reconstruct the great archaeological site of Teotihuacan, and to conduct an anthropological exploration of the surrounding population. The results of the project were published in the lavishly produced and illustrated, *The Population of the Valley of Teotihuacan* (1922). At one stroke, Gamio succeeded in installing Indian civilisation as the historic foundation of Mexican culture and society, since the imposing scale of the site's monuments elicited immediate comparison with the pyramids of Egypt. Not content with mere reconstruction of the past, Gamio wrote a popular guide designed to encourage tourism and encouraged local artisans to sell their wares at the site. Equally importantly, the survey's exploration of land tenure in the district revealed that seven haciendas occupied most of the land, the peasantry clustered in independent villages. To resolve this problem, he advocated agrarian reform, endowing each village with sufficient land, its ownership to be vested in the community. Alluding to 'pseudo-Bolshevik leaders' who proposed the formation of Mexican soviets, Gamio justified his programme by appeal to pre-hispanic and colonial precedent, praising 'the system of cooperativism *(mutualismo)* or rural communism, but not Bolshevism'. So also, he initiated a campaign to revive popular crafts, in textiles, ceramics, lacquer wares and metal work, arguing that this 'national industry' should be promoted by the government to provide much needed rural employment. In defending the achievements of native civilisation, he criticised the hegemony of neo-classical taste and asserted that it was on an Indian basis that a new national art should be formed, an all important project since art was 'one of the great bases of nationalism'. But although Gamio insisted that the bulk of the Mexican population still preserved elements of ancient Indian culture and employed the resources of the revolutionary state to promote that culture, in the last resort he favoured the assimilation of the peasantry into the modern nation he strove to form. He sustained the longstanding Liberal contempt for popular Catholicism and favoured the replacement of Indian languages by Spanish. In the long run, folk culture was doomed to disappear and the task of government was to rescue the native peasantry from their poverty and ignorance and thereby incorporate them into the national community.[35]

So all-pervasive was the influence of nationalism in revolutionary Mexico that Positivists and Social Darwinists elaborated their own variant doctrines. In *Los grandes problemas nacionales* (1909) Andrés Molina Enríquez applied the evolutionary theory of Ernest Haeckal to assert that the Mexican mestizo formed a new race of man, endowed with its own character and inner force, which by reason of its historical adaptation to the American environment was destined to thrive and multiply. As much Asian as European, the mestizos were

---

[35] Manuel Gamio (ed.), *La Población del Valle de Teotihuacán*, facsimile edn., 5 vols. (Mexico, 1979), Vol. I, pp. lxxxl-v, xvii; see also D.A. Brading, 'Manuel Gamio and Official Indigenism in Mexico', *Bulletin of Latin American Research*, Vol. 7 (1988), pp. 75-88.

distinguished 'neither for their beauty nor for their culture, nor in general by the refinement of races of advanced evolution, but rather by the conditions of their incomparable adaptation to the environment, by the qualities of their powerful animal force'. From the condition of social pariahs, *desheredados*, the mestizos had fought their way to political dominance. Moreover, such was the biological force of this race, that in any longterm battle for survival against more evolved societies, which is to say, against the United States, it was destined to conquer. Within Mexico, only the mestizos could be counted as true Mexicans. By reason of their European ancestry, the Creoles remained an exotic flower grafted onto the main trunk of the Mexican race, always bound by sentiment, culture and custom to their overseas antecedents, thus forming a perpetual fifth column, their frequent marriages and business partnerships with foreign migrants and investors a source of political danger. As for the indians, Molina Enríquez agreed with Gamio that the *pueblo* was the true *patria*, their local attachments and languages leaving them untouched by any loyalty to the nation or its state.[36] One consequence of the primacy of racial considerations was that Molina Enríquez openly defended the necessity of authoritarian government in Mexico, asserting that for both Indians and mestizos 'the spontaneous and material form of government is dictatorship'. Indeed, as late as the 1930s, he defended the achievements of Porfirio Díaz, insisting that his regime 'had encountered in its structure and in its very stability the definitive form of national government'. Yet he combined these apparently reactionary sentiments with a strong commitment to agrarian reform, dismissing the traditional hacienda as a feudal institution, the chief obstacle to social justice and economic progress. He was the intellectual author of article 27 of the 1917 Constitution, which defined the nation as the primordial owner of all land within the territory of the republic, demanded the destruction of latifundia, and restored communal ownership of land to Indian villages. When this article was later attacked for its 'outright communism', Molina Enríquez argued that philosophically the text simply asserted the Comtean principle that the rights of society precede and are superior to the rights of the individual.[37] In practice, the article simply restored to the Mexican nation the rights once enjoyed by the Spanish Crown and re-introduced the dual principles of individual and collective ownership that had been so wisely sustained by the Crown during the colonial period. Here, then, was a potent and highly original broth of positivism, social Darwinism and radical nationalism, all marshalled to serve and justify the projects of the revolutionary state.

As the example of Molina Enríquez demonstrates, the flowering of nationalism in Latin America during the first decades of the twentieth century had several quite distinct intellectual sources. Romantic idealism bloomed

---

[36] Andrés Molina Enríquez, *Los grandes problemas nacionales (1909) y otros textos 1911-1919*, prólogo de Arnaldo Córdova (Mexico, 1978), pp. 34, 274-7, 349, 356.

[37] Andrés Molina Enríquez, *La revolución agraria en México*, 2nd. edn. (Mexico, 1976), pp. 324, 384-98; Molina Enríquez, *Los grandes problemas nacionales y otros textos*, pp. 465-78; Brading, *Prophecy and Myth*, pp. 64-71.

alongside radical positivism, and indeed in some cases both were embraced simultaneously by ideologues disenchanted with classical liberalism. But although there was widespread rejection of the achievements of the nineteenth century, it was rare for the icons of republican patriotism to be expelled from national pantheons. Indeed, the figures of Bolívar, San Martín and Juárez loomed ever larger, their continued presence testimony of the essential continuity between republican patriotism and popular nationalism. Is it too much to suggest that Comtean positivism was the chief bridge between liberalism and nationalism? Had not Comte condemned parliamentary forms of government as an idle charade, which should be replaced by a regime dominated by bankers and industrialists? He also advocated an alliance between intellectuals and workers, with the aim of avoiding socialism. In this scheme, intellectuals re-enacted the role of the Catholic priesthood, justifying the inevitability of an unequal distribution of income, but insisting on the necessity of the state ensuring social justice.[38] In Latin America positivists tended to accept authoritarian regimes but were quick to fix upon the danger of socialist propaganda among the masses.

The degree to which state-building could be justified by such Comtean doctrines can be observed in Brazil, where on introducing his five year plan in 1940, President Getúlio Vargas declared: 'we feel that the old systems and antiquated formulae have entered into decline.. The State, therefore, should assume the obligation of organising the productive forces, to provide the people with all that is necessary for collective welfare....The era of improvident liberalism, sterile demagoguery, useless individualism and disorder has passed'. The scion of a political machine in Rio Grande do Sul, which from its seizure of power in 1889 had been inspired by positivism, in 1937 Vargas established the Estado Novo, a regime which relied on the federal army to provide a cadre of officers to administer the state enterprises which he founded to promote industrial development. In practical politics he suppressed both the communist-led ANL and the semi-fascist Integralists, relying on rural *coroneis* to control the countryside and on state-promoted labour unions to organise the urban workers. His brand of autarchic industrial development was strongly supported by the army which hailed the project as the foundation of national security.[39] No doubt, nationalist doctrines of romantic origin flowered as much in Brazil as in Spanish America, but the achievements of the Vargas regime suggest that statebuilding and economic modernisation could be undertaken and justified by ideas and measures that emerged from within the mainstream of Western liberalism and its conservative counterpart. The state in Latin America preceded the formation of nations and it renewed its strength by intervention in both the

---

[38] Auguste Comte, *Appeal to Conservatives* (London, 1889), pp. 127-50.

[39] Citation from John W.F. Dulles, *Vargas of Brazil* (Austin, 1967), p. 210; for positivism see Joseph L. Love, *Rio Grande do Sul and Brazilian Regionalism 1882-1930* (Stanford, 1971), pp. 26-36, 45; Frederick M. Nunn, *Yesterday's Soldiers. European Military Professionalism in South America, 1890-1940* (Lincoln, Neb., 1983), pp. 255-68.

economy and society, much as was the case in Europe, the political bureaucracy seeking to deploy its power and resources in a dual struggle against foreign imperialism and domestic socialism. It is this dual struggle which drove the diverse regimes which dominated Mexico, Argentina and Brazil to promote industrialisation and to organise the masses. Whether nationalism can be interpreted as a causative agent or as a justificatory fiction still requires more discussion and analysis than is as yet possible.

IV

The purpose of this paper has been to argue that both independence and the first phase of state-building in Spanish America were justified by the familiar theories of European liberalism, which is to say, by the doctrines of popular sovereignty and the right to self-government. But this type of political theory was soon supplemented by classical republicanism, which found expression in the cult of patriotic heroes and the elevation of the *patria* as the focus of social identity. It was only at the start of the twentieth century that nationalism emerged in Latin America, drawing upon a variegated range of sources, and often still uncertain as to the identity of the nation in question. That so many intellectuals accepted the *patria grande*, i.e. all Spanish America, as their true nation, indicates the debility of local forms of nationalism. In the first instance, nationalists such as Rodó and Vasconcelos reacted against modernity, embodied in the United States, and appealed to history and culture to preserve their countries from US domination. But the forces of modernisation already operating, thanks to foreign investment, trade and immigration, drove nationalists to enlist in the grand task of state-building. Before forming a nation, it was necessary to build a state with power and resources sufficient to promote economic development and social welfare, with the aim of incorporating the peasantry into a literate, modern society. Whereas in Europe nationalist doctrines often merged into outright fascism, in Latin America these doctrines in part drove the political bureaucracy to create powerful states which sought to incorporate the masses into their structure, thereby pre-empting the rise of socialist or fascist parties. In the last resort, the relations between nationalist ideology and the practical politics of state-building was ambiguous and varied from country to country – and still requires a great deal of further analysis and discussion.

Printed in the United States
1301800001B/21-78